PROMISES FULFILLED

A LEADER'S GUIDE FOR SUPPORTING ENGLISH LEARNERS

MARGARITA ESPINO CALDERÓN
SHAWN SLAKK
with HECTOR MONTENEGRO

Solution Tree | Press

555 North Morton Street
Bloomington, IN 47404
800.733.6786 (toll free) / 812.336.7700
FAX: 812.336.7790

email: info@SolutionTree.com
SolutionTree.com

Visit **go.SolutionTree.com/EL** to download the free reproducibles in this book.

Printed in the United States of America

Library of Congress Control Number: 2016954303

Solution Tree
Jeffrey C. Jones, CEO
Edmund M. Ackerman, President

Solution Tree Press
President: Douglas M. Rife
Editorial Director: Tonya Maddox Cupp
Managing Production Editor: Caroline Weiss
Senior Editor: Amy Rubenstein
Senior Production Editor: Todd Brakke
Copy Chief: Sarah Payne-Mills
Proofreader: Elisabeth Abrams
Text and Cover Designer: Abigail Bowen
Editorial Assistants: Jessi Finn and Kendra Slayton

ACKNOWLEDGMENTS

We would like to thank Douglas Rife, president and publisher of Solution Tree Press, for his guidance with this book, which the field had been asking us to publish! We are most appreciative of the editorial staff and their prompt and valuable responses. Moreover, Claudia Wheatley, content specialist and author liaison, has been an inspiration to us as we set our professional development experiences into writing.

Additionally, we owe many principals and district administrators for the opportunities they gave us to test the concepts and components described in this book. We are particularly indebted to Judy Radford, ESL Professional Development Coordinator, Virginia State Department of Education; Heidi Ramirez, Chief Academic Officer, and Kori Hamner, Director of Support and Professional Development, from Shelby County Schools, Tennessee; and Andrés Enriquez from the Carnegie Corporation of New York for encouraging and funding the empirical research on ExC-ELL.

We would also like to thank our families and colleagues who make it possible for us to do the work we do and help to make it enjoyable.

Solution Tree Press would like to thank the following reviewers:

Zhaneta Liti
English Language
  Coordinator, East
Massachusetts Department of
  Elementary and Secondary
  Education
Malden, Massachusetts

Richard Long
Executive Director
Learning First Alliance
Washington, DC

Amy Swick
Continuous School
  Improvement Coordinator
  of ELL/Bilingual Programs
Appleton Area School District
Appleton, Wisconsin

Visit **go.SolutionTree.com/EL** to download the
free reproducibles in this book.

TABLE OF CONTENTS

CHAPTER 3

English Language Development and Social and Emotional Skills. 51

CHAPTER 4

Professional Development Components . . . 65

CHAPTER 5
Professional Coaching in the Classroom . . 85

CHAPTER 6
Sustaining a Quality Implementation 99

CHAPTER 7
Whole-School Approach to Success for
ELs (and All Other Students) 113

APPENDIX A
Recommended Books and Online
Resources 125

APPENDIX B
Glossary of EL Categories 127

References and Resources 133

Index 143

ABOUT THE AUTHORS

 **Margarita Espino Calderón, PhD,** is professor emerita and senior research scientist at the Johns Hopkins University School of Education. She has conducted research, training, and curriculum development for teaching language, reading comprehension, and content knowledge to K–12 English learners. Her work has focused on effective instructional processes, two-way and dual-language programs, teacher learning communities, and professional development for schools with language minority populations and striving adolescent readers. Dr. Calderón's research has been supported by the New York Carnegie Corporation Foundation, U.S. Department of Education, U.S. Department of Labor, National Institutes of Health, and the Texas Education Agency.

A native of Juárez, Mexico, Dr. Calderón is a recognized expert in education with more than one hundred publications to her credit. She is a respected member of several panels and national committees, and she has been welcomed internationally as a visiting lecturer. Dr. Calderón has created and directed her own international institutes for administrators, teachers, and parents. She has experience as a classroom teacher, bilingual program director, professional development coordinator, professor of educational leadership graduate programs, and bilingual teacher supervisor.

Dr. Calderón earned a doctorate in multicultural education, applied linguistics, and organizational development through a joint doctorate program at Claremont Graduate University and San Diego State University.

Shawn Slakk, Chief Learning Officer for ABCDS&S Consulting, works with teachers, administrators, schools, and state agencies to offer strategies and support for multilingual learners and their classmates, in grades K–12 and adults. He is an author and developer of professional learning sessions for all levels of educators, focusing on whole-school implementation, administrative support, and coaching.

Shawn additionally partners with the Center for Applied Linguistics (CAL) to offer professional learning opportunities in SIOP. He has over thirty years of experience in teaching and administration for ESL, bilingual, and Spanish instruction across all grade levels and curricula. He expertly helps teachers, schools, or districts infuse language acquisition skills to help multilingual learners succeed with literacy and content mastery via professional learning, school leadership, program analysis, and compliance strategies.

Throughout his career, in addition to founding ABCDS&S Consulting, Shawn has held leadership positions with the Massachusetts Department of Elementary and Secondary Education, Charlotte Mecklenburg Schools, and Guilford County Schools. As the Coordinator of Rethinking Equity and Teaching for English Language Learners (RETELL) for the Massachusetts Department of Elementary and Secondary Education, he and his staff developed, evaluated, and refined the Sheltered English Instruction endorsement courses for administrators and classroom teachers. This included work with instructional strategies, lesson delivery, and assessment to support teachers of English language learners at all levels.

Hector Montenegro, EdD, president and CEO of Montenegro Consulting Group, is an associate for Margarita Calderón & Associates. He is an internationally recognized keynote and motivational speaker, appearing at conferences, conventions, universities, schools, and special events around the world. He provides training on instructional strategies for English learners and leadership development for administrators and instructional coaches, and he specializes in the teacher coaching process through the use of technology, video recording, web-based platforms, and observation protocols. Dr. Montenegro is also a senior district advisor for the Collaborative for Academic, Social, and Emotional Learning (CASEL) and works with districts on systemic implementation of social and emotional learning.

Dr. Montenegro began his teaching career in 1975 in San Jose, California, where he taught mathematics at the junior and senior high school levels. He later taught and was an assistant principal in Washington, DC, and a junior high principal and a high school principal in Virginia. He also served as chief of staff of the District of Columbia Public Schools before moving to Texas, where he served as a principal and an area superintendent in Austin, deputy superintendent for instructional services in Dallas, and superintendent of schools for three school districts in Texas: San Marcos Consolidated Independent School District, Ysleta Independent School District, and Arlington Independent School District. In addition, Dr. Montenegro was an area superintendent for the San Diego School District in California. He has received numerous awards, including the 2007 National Technology Savvy Superintendents Award, the 2006 Texas Association for Bilingual Education (TABE) Honoree Award for Public Education, the 2006 League of United Latin American Citizens (LULAC) National Distinguished Educator Award for Commitment in Education, the 2006 Texas Computer Education Association Technology Administrator of the Year Award, and the 2005 LULAC National Educator of the Year Award. He obtained his master's degree from Stanford University and doctoral degree from the University of Texas at Austin.

To book Margarita Calderón, Shawn Slakk, or Hector Montenegro for professional development, contact pd@SolutionTree.com.

INTRODUCTION

Just Who Are My English Learners, and How Do I Serve Them?

Limited English Proficient (LEP)

Academic definition: Individuals who do not speak English as their primary language and who have a limited ability to read, speak, write, or understand English can be limited English proficient, or LEP. These individuals may be entitled to language assistance with respect to a particular type of service, benefit, or encounter (Limited English Proficiency, n.d.).

Friendly definition: Any non-native English learner (EL) who is learning English as an additional language. *English learner* is now the preferred notation.

If your school does not yet have a student identified as limited English proficient or an English learner, it soon will. Are you ready?

ELs will invariably come to your school with a variety of abilities, proficiency levels, content competencies, cultural and educational backgrounds, and instructional and social and emotional needs. They will need instruction in how to read, write, and comprehend English. ELs, with minor exceptions, are already literate or semiliterate in a language. In fact, many are highly literate in several languages. Many are equally educated in the core content of mathematics,

1

science, social studies, and language arts as their native English-speaking peers.

We crafted this book specifically to help administrators and teacher leaders coach and support teachers in preK–12 classrooms to help and support English learners. Within the next few pages, we help you get to know who your ELs are and discuss the best ways for you to identify and serve them.

The goals for this book are to help readers identify, classify, and serve their ELs while complying with federal laws and guidelines. In addition, it will help schools and districts educate their staff in how to integrate evidence-based instructional strategies that apply to ELs and their non-EL classmates. Having experienced success with schools that implement these instructional strategies school-wide, in this book we recommend a whole-school approach, offer steps to implement it, and highlight the benefits all your students and teaching staff will derive.

Types of English Learners

The overall category—and the U.S. government's former way of identifying EL students—is *limited English proficient*. Throughout this book, we refer to LEP students as English learners or ELs. You may also hear those in the profession call them English language learners (ELLs) or English as a second language (ESL) students. To tweak a William Shakespeare quote, an English learner by any other name is still a student who needs explicit instruction in learning and using English as an additional language.

English Learners From the United States

It is interesting to note that Title III includes Native American and Alaska Native children in the LEP category. Others are surprised perhaps to learn that a solid majority of ELs are natural-born citizens of the United States.

Educators identify ELs in many subcategories: newcomers, long-term ELs (LT-ELs), highly schooled newcomers (HSNs), migrant ELs (M-ELs), students with interrupted formal education (SIFE) or students with limited or interrupted formal education (SLIFE), refugees, immigrant students, ethnic minorities, forever ELs, ELs with special education services (SE-ELs), and, at times, language minority students (LMs). That's a lot of subcategories and acronyms! The good news is that you don't need to commit each and every one of them to memory, but rather keep in mind that these categories exist when assessing students, and reference them as needed. Because each student is an individual, students may have characteristics of several of these subgroups and, as such, need accurate identification so that they receive the services that best suit their unique needs.

In appendix B (page 127), we include a miniglossary that can help you make sense of the alphabet soup that is the LEP world. We suggest you locate it now and perhaps bookmark it for quick reference. It does not list all of the terms districts use to identify ELs, but it does cover the most common categories. Throughout the rest of this guide, we add to the definitions related to services, assessment, data, strategies, and compliance.

English Learners in Your Classrooms

ELs are entitled to additional services by the Every Student Succeeds Act (ESSA, 2016), formerly known as the Elementary and Secondary Education Act (ESEA) Title III—Language Instruction for Limited English Proficient and Immigrant Students. These services exist specifically for the purpose of learning English in an academic setting, thus enabling students to become productive participants in their schools and communities. The first step along this process is to accurately identify an EL student. Once identified, your next *big step* is to enlist everyone in implementing a whole-school approach to ensure success for ELs as well as all other students.

When implementing the whole-school approach, we suggest that all members of the staff work as a whole to educate the ELs. This includes supporting and coaching instructional support staff, supplemental educational staff, facilitators, coaches, and administration in research-based strategies. By adopting the attitude that all members of the staff have a part in educating and ensuring success for all learners, schools succeed. When we train all members in the same strategies, and administration can inspect against expectation and coach, as well as evaluate that target strategies and instructional goals are being implemented, schools succeed. When all processes, strategies, goals, and expectations are unified throughout a school, schools succeed.

How Do I Start Identifying My ELs?

Identifying ELs when they enter your school or district is imperative. The Office for Civil Rights at the U.S. Department of Education (USDOE) and the Civil Rights Division at the U.S. Department of Justice (USDOJ) recommend that every district has a process to identify entering LEP students—typically in the form of a home language survey (USDOJ, 2015b). Many schools and districts have a family welcome center or the equivalent through which all students wishing to enroll in the school district register. If your system has such a process, great! You are halfway there. If your school lacks a sufficient process for EL identification, using a home language survey to identify those students whose native language is not English is a good place to start. A home language survey asks four simple questions.

1. What language do you speak with your child at home?

2. What language does your child speak at home with you?

3. What language does your child speak with his or her friends?

4. What language did your child speak when learning how to talk?

If a parent answers any language other than English for any of the four questions, the student should be screened for his or her English language development (ELD) level.

If you'd like to see specific examples of a home language survey in practice, a quick Internet search will provide you with several good examples. The Office of Superintendent of Public Instruction for the state of Washington provides an excellent example as well as an explanation of how it helps students (http://www.k12.wa.us/MigrantBilingual/pubdocs/HLS/HLSEnglish.pdf).

To see how you can best integrate a home language survey into a standard registration process, look at the example of the Charlotte-Mecklenburg Schools, in Charlotte, North Carolina (http://www.cms .k12.nc.us/cmsdepartments/StudentPlacement/Documents/2013-14 %20Enrollment%20Packet%20(English).pdf). This district's International Center also provides a good example of inclusive ELservices including but not limited to just the registration and screening process (www.cms.k12.nc.us/cmsdepartments/ci/els /ic/Pages/default.aspx). The Family Registration and Orientation Center, in Spokane Public Schools, Spokane, Washington and the International Welcome Center of Albemarle County Public Schools, in Charlottesville, Virginia are also good examples (www .spokaneschools.org/Page/1505 or www2.k12albemarle.org/dept /instruction/esol/Pages/default.aspx).

Many times, instead of enrolling through an International Center, EL students enroll directly at the school they will attend, where it's possible for their EL status to go unidentified. This puts the burden of responsibility for identifying these students directly on the school.

Regardless of the location for registration, a very specific process must occur. Those who are responsible for the intake process must receive training to recognize students who may need ESL services. If a school system identifies a student as knowing, speaking, using, or hearing a language other than English in the home, or with family and friends, it must screen the student. This requires that the school have adequate translation and assistance resources available to accomplish this screening. Failing to properly screen the incoming students means that the entire district is out of compliance with ESSA.

Schools that identify students as ELs, and thus receive ESL services, must screen those students and inform their parents of this identification within thirty days of enrollment (USDOJ, 2015b). The time frame for identifying possible EL students during the school year is typically ten to fourteen days. Because there is no hierarchy of ELs, we use the honeycomb graphic shown in figure I.1 (page 6) as a visual to keep in mind that, while different ELs may have different needs, they are equal members of the classroom, just as the general education non-EL students are.

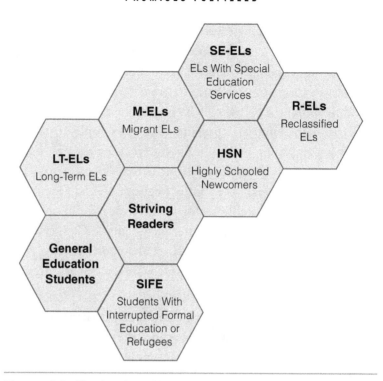

Figure I.1: Understanding the different subcategories of English learners.

After the registration process, it's a good practice to check students' records to see if they previously received or currently receive EL services. This records review serves as a useful double-check, ensuring the student receives all the services to which he or she is entitled. If the school has already identified the student, the screening process is unnecessary. Services commence immediately based on the student's records. If the student's records indicate that he or she has exited LEP status, the school needs to monitor him or her for two years following the status change. We expect the ESSA to soon require four years of monitoring.

Once the school system identifies an EL student, it must notify the parents that their child will participate in ESL service. This notification must include the reason for identifying the student, the student's ELD level, how the school determined his or her ELD level, the services the student will receive, the manner of assessment for exiting, how ESL services will dovetail with other services a student might receive (special education, speech, and so on), and the options available for the student to receive services, including the right to decline supplemental services.

Parents may opt out of or waive direct ESL services (USDOJ, 2015b). The school system should inform parents who decline supplemental services that it still identifies their child as EL and will require him or her to participate in all federally mandated assessments in a language he or she understands, potentially with accommodations, until the student exits EL status (USDOJ, 2015b).

This process requires diligence to ensure that parents fully understand that waiving or opting out of supplemental services does not release the local educational agency from documenting the student's ELD progress, nor does it remove the student from LEP status. Equally important is that the local education agency (LEA), the federal government's label for a school district (or division) and its agents and representatives (schools, staff, administration, and teachers), understands the added impetus to provide EL support and explicit instruction to the student whose family declined supplemental services.

Once you've identified your EL students, you must take them through the process of assessing their needs, setting a plan for their specific educational needs, and assessing their progress over time.

How Do I Assess My Potential ELs?

After the identification process, potential ELs need to take an English language placement test. For the purposes of discussion, we use the WIDA-ACCESS Placement Test (W-APT) as an example of a placement screener. The W-APT has a related annual English language development assessment, ACCESS for ELLs 2.0. WIDA is a consortium of thirty-eight states that offers a unified set of English language assessments and provides a data clearinghouse to member states of the consortium for those LEP students who have been screened and later assessed on their English language progress. (For transparency, one of the authors is a certified WIDA trainer, but that organization does not compensate the authors in any fashion. We simply use WIDA and the tools it provides as an example of a recognized process that facilitates the identification and service of ELs.)

Each LEA is at liberty to choose a screener. However, this screener must evaluate a student's English language ability in the four language domains—(1) listening, (2) speaking, (3) reading, and (4) writing—at the student's grade level. It must also evaluate the requisite components of English language usage and grammar. If the school administers the W-APT or other screener and does not identify the student as an EL student, the process has concluded— the student is not EL and as such does not qualify for additional English language learning services.

What Do I Do After LEP Identification?

When a school identifies a student as EL, the next step is to determine the level of service. As an example of ESL direct instructional guidelines, we reference and synthesize into the following list a portion of the consent decree between Boston Public Schools (BPS) and the U.S. Department of Justice for the 2010 to 2011 school year (USDOJ, 2010). We selected this source as an acceptable starting point for adequate services for ELs.

- Group ELs for ESL instruction by their English proficiency level or comparable, consecutive levels of English proficiency.
- Require at least one class period of ESL instruction.
- Provide ESL instruction in a self-contained class of ELs, a pull-out setting, or a push-in setting in an English language arts class.
- Determine direct service hours by ELD level as currently required in Massachusetts.

In this book, we chose Massachusetts as an example of how a State Educational Agency, in compliance with the United States Department of Justice, chose to move forward to serve its increasing population of LEP students. In 2016, according to the Massachusettes Department of Elementary and Secondary Education State Report Card, ELs comprise 9 percent of the population. A quick review of Massachusetts's 516 public and private LEAs shows that the LEP population by LEA ranges from just over 30 percent in Boston Public Schools to less than 0.1 percent in LEAs such as Berkley or Pentucket. Regardless of total percentage, an LEA is required to provide services to its EL population, whether there are thousands or only one.

With this in mind, after identifying a student as qualifying for ESL services, implementing a plan of action guided by the English language development level of the student must take place. Using the collected data from the screening tool used informs the LEA as to the level of service required for each student. For those LEAs who use WIDA's W-APT, the following list provides guidelines to those levels of service. For those LEAs who do not use the W-APT, reviewing the following levels of service based on a student's level— be it novice, intermediate, or advanced—will help to inform the LEA as to an adequate level of service.

- **Foundational (WIDA levels 1 and 2):** At this level, a licensed ESL teacher delivers at least two to three periods (not less than forty-five minutes each) per day of direct ESL instruction.
- **Transitional (WIDA levels 3, 4, and 5):** At this level, a licensed ESL teacher delivers at least one period (not less than forty-five minutes) per day of direct ESL instruction.
- **Reaching (WIDA level 6):** Schools should no longer classify students at WIDA level 6 as ELs; they should participate in the general education program alongside fluent or native English-speaking peers. The school system must monitor students' progress for four years after it removes their EL classification. Such students should also receive additional support and services if needed.

  Other states require similar time frames. For the rest of the instructional day, a teacher who has undergone professional development focusing on academic language instructional strategies, such as ExC-ELL or Massachusetts's sheltered English instruction endorsement, should teach ELs.

Once you understand the level of service the EL student requires, you can establish whether you have enough qualified ESL teachers to serve the LEA, begin instruction, and monitor EL progress over time.

How Do I Assess EL Progress?

At least once a year, as mandated by Section 1111 (b) (7) of the No Child Left Behind Act of 2001, LEAs must assess their ELs' progress. States and groups that belong to the WIDA Consortium use the ACCESS for ELLs 2.0 Summative Assessment. Each LEA outlines the exiting criteria for students who have achieved an adequate level of English proficiency to remain successful with classroom academics on a commensurate level with their never-EL peers. A quick Google search for LEP exit criteria provides numerous examples of how various states determine the exiting criteria of LEP students.

Remember, assessment and services do not end here. An EL who exits EL status becomes *formerly limited English proficient* and the school must monitor him or her for a minimum of two years (soon, four years) to ensure that he or she has indeed obtained the necessary proficiency to achieve academic success (USDOJ, 2015b).

Who Do I Need to Involve in Serving My ELs?

Just whose job is it to offer an EL student the support he or she needs? Short answer: Everyone's!

Realistically? You should involve any educator—particularly a school principal or district administrator—who is a part of an EL's life, academic or otherwise, in seeing that the student succeeds. All teachers teach language and literacy, even high school content teachers. Schools should also directly involve parents. In addition, the community is an important partner in helping all students succeed by helping support initiatives that accelerate achievement (USDOE Newcomer Toolkit, 2016).

Within the LEA and, more pointedly, at the building level, all teachers who teach an EL should receive professional development to advance their skills in teaching academic language to ELs. This includes not only core subject area teachers but also enrichment, supplemental services, tutoring, electives, and advanced placement teachers. All should be highly qualified to provide academic language instruction.

In conjunction with professional development sessions, working within professional team structures, establishing common planning and lesson assessment, and providing development time all strengthen the teachers' learning process. Administrator support is key to these planning and assessment activities. Educators who form a team development structure and have common planning time report to us that they have great self-efficacy and confidence to work successfully with ELs.

LEAs with professional learning communities (PLCs) should explicitly include EL data, as many schools throughout the country now do. The schools where we work have specific PLC teams devoted to including ELs and serving ELs through whole-school structures. This is a new shift for PLCs. They also establish teacher learning communities (TLCs) where teachers focus on EL learning progressions, the effects of their instruction on ELs, and continuous collegial learning about instruction for ELs. TLCs are cross-curricular and vertically span grade levels. Subsequent chapters detail how to support and sustain team development focused on ELs.

How This Book Supports English Learners

Now that you have a basic understanding of the process and work involved in identifying and supporting EL students, let's take a specific look at how this book will help ensure that you and your teachers are able to fulfill your promises to EL students.

In chapter 1, we discuss legal requirements for educators regarding ELs. To do so, we explore the guidelines from the U.S. Department of Justice and the Office of Civil Rights. We also look at where funding will come from. In chapter 2, we dig deep into the instructional components, from professional development to lesson planning for preteaching vocabulary, and developing reading comprehension and academic writing skills. Chapter 3 covers the development of social-emotional learning. Under that umbrella, we look at activities and instructional practices that cultivate cultural responsiveness. Chapter 4 explores in more detail how professional development fits into the big picture. We provide research on supporting professional development and show what effective professional development looks like in action. In chapter 5, we focus on observing the EL classroom, including the logistics for expert coaches' visits and self-reflection for coaches. Chapter 6 is all about implementation. We dig into ways of transforming training into classroom learning and emphasize the importance of celebrating. Finally, chapter 7 discusses the whole-school approach to EL success and that of all students.

At the end of each chapter, you will find discussion questions to consider for yourself, your staff, and your collaboration team. Do note that we have intentionally made the outside margin of this guide extra wide so that you have room to make notes and plan for your school's implementation with your colleagues. This book also includes a few other recurring elements.

 This *Be on the Lookout* icon signifies spots in chapter 1 (page xx) where we propose tips or guide you to the chapter where we elaborate on how to structure your plan, implement it, and assess progress.

Feature Box

We use feature boxes to quickly highlight ancillary or tangential information to the topic at hand.

We end the book with two appendices: (1) a list of recommended books for further reading, and (2) a glossary of terms.

Discussion Questions

Consider the following.

- Who are our ELs? How do we know who our ELs are? What do we need to change or implement in our identification process?
- How are we serving our ELs? Does our program of services live up to the expectations of the U.S. Department of Justice?

CHAPTER 1

What We Are Required to Do for ELs

Adequate

Academic definition: (1) Sufficient for a specific requirement; also, barely sufficient or satisfactory; (2) lawfully and reasonably sufficient

Friendly definition: The necessary amount to succeed

Typically many local educational agencies and states relegated all duties relevant to ELs to the ESL teacher or the EL coordinator (Calderón, 2011a). The ESL teacher or coordinator screened, placed, assessed, and kept track of ELs and exited ELs from EL programs. In many cases, ESL teachers and coordinators were the only ones who explicitly taught these students—that is, until there were so many EL students that change became necessary.

Initiatives from the Department of Justice and Office of Civil Rights (part of the U.S. Department of Education) helped pave the way for that change (USDOJ & USDOE, 2015a, 2015b). The *Dear Colleague Letters* that the DOJ and OCR sent to all LEAs across the United States described the regulations while providing guidelines to meet the letter of the law concerning EL services. This chapter summarizes the information from the DOJ and OCR reports, letters, and guiding tools to help LEAs confirm what they have on hand and what they might need to revisit.

Every Student Succeeds Act

Concomitant with the DOJ and OCR *Dear Colleague Letters*, the Every Student Succeeds Act (ESSA, 2016) was enacted to benefit all students, but it calls for changes and modifications that specifically expand access to and benefit greatly the education of ELs, as well as homeless children, students with special needs, children of migratory families, and Native American students (all of whom might include ELs). The goals of ESSA include:

- Holding all students to high academic standards that prepare them for success in college and careers
- Ensuring accountability by guaranteeing that when students fall behind, states redirect resources into what works to help them and their schools improve, with a particular focus on the very lowest-performing schools, high schools with high dropout rates, and schools with achievement gaps
- Empowering state and local decision makers to develop their own strong systems for school improvement based on evidence, rather than imposing cookie-cutter federal solutions like the No Child Left Behind Act (2008)
- Reducing the often onerous burden of testing on students and teachers, making sure that tests don't crowd out teaching and learning, without sacrificing clear, annual information parents and educators need to make sure students are learning
- Providing more students access to high-quality preschool
- Establishing new resources for proven strategies that spur reform and drive opportunity and better outcomes for U.S. students

In short, ESSA expects that ELs, along with all other students, receive a well-rounded education based on college and career-ready standards (ESSA, 2016). It expands the areas of STEM (science, technology, engineering, and mathematics) to include the arts, thus changing the acronym STEM to STEAM (*A* for *arts*). This benefits ELs tremendously because they can begin participating with their artistic talents immediately without having to wait for their language skills to reach a certain level.

Finally, rigorous accountability for all students undergirds all instructional efforts. A smart and balanced approach to testing de-emphasizes high-stakes assessment practices that previously punished ELs. Instead, schools and districts can establish a more sensible and sensitive process of assessment.

Key Federal Guidelines and Requirements

Federal law requirements and guidelines are the foundation of EL instruction. These requirements are the first item to discuss with the whole school staff. A quick review of them, in conjunction with the school's own practices, helps put existing accomplishments out in front where everyone can see them. Sometimes, it is only the administration and the ESL or ELD specialist who are thoroughly aware of, and actively involved in, all EL issues. As we established from the outset, it is everyone's responsibility to support EL students.

The 2015 *Dear Colleague Letter* and the Office of English Language Acquisition English Learner Toolkit available from the U.S. Department of Justice and the Office for Civil Rights establish ten key requirements that help schools ensure quality education and equity for ELs (USDOE, 2015).

10 Key Requirements for Supporting ELs

Go to www2.ed.gov/about/offices/list/ocr/ellresources .html to access the Office of English Language Acquisition English Learner Toolkit.

1. Identifying all English learner students
2. Providing English learners with a language assistance program
3. Staffing and supporting an EL program
4. Providing meaningful access to all curricular and extracurricular programs
5. Creating an inclusive environment and avoiding unnecessary segregation

6. Addressing English learners with disabilities

7. Serving English learners who opt out of EL programs

8. Monitoring and exiting English learners

9. Evaluating the effectiveness of a district's EL program

10. Ensuring meaningful communication with limited English proficient parents

In reviewing these requirements, keep the word *equity* in the forefront of your mind. In this context, equity means that ELs must have equal opportunities to succeed academically and must participate in all educational activities—including extracurricular or advanced placement. ELs are part of the school's student body. They can participate meaningfully and equally in educational programs when there are specific structures and processes in place.

Establishing equity is critical because the Office for Civil Rights examines a broad range of information sources that address the ten guidelines when assessing whether a school or district discriminates based on race in providing access to strong teaching and instruction for ELs (USDOJ & USDOE, 2015a). As a result of this examination, the consent decree with Boston Public Schools (USDOJ, 2010), the recommendations provided to Boston Public Schools and the Massachusetts' Department of Elementary and Secondary Education (Calderón, 2010–2014), and other similar DOJ reviews in conjunction with the requirements of ESSA, the DOJ's January 2015 *Dear Colleague Letter* created and disseminated a variety of data related to the teachers, leaders, and staff in an LEA's schools (USDOJ & USDOE, 2015a). These sources contain data on the following characteristics and qualifications of teachers: teachers' licensure and certification status, whether teachers have completed appropriate training and professional development, whether teachers are inexperienced, whether they are teaching subjects outside of their field, and other indicators of disparities in access to strong teachers. Moreover, these ten requirements help school staffs gauge challenges, progress, and success.

We wrote in the Introduction about general guidelines for identifying EL students. Federal guidelines also have a big role in this process because they mandate having procedures in place for timely and accurate identification of ELs, beginning with a home language survey. Each of the following sections provides the exact text for one of the ten federal requirements for supporting ELs. After each requirement description from the DOJ and OCR, we propose some tips or guide you to the chapter where we elaborate on how to include the requirements in your plan, implement them, and assess their progress.

DOJ and OCR Requirement 1: Identifying and Assessing Students

Federal Requirement:

Have procedures in place for timely and accurate identification of ELs beginning with a Home Language Survey that gathers information about the student's language background and the student's home language if it is other than English.

Sometimes, parents do not want to admit they speak another language at home for fear that their child will be singled out for being an EL. If so, help parents and guardians understand the importance of EL programs and services. Schools might need to revisit their processes for reaching out to parents and guardians to ensure accuracy of information, delivery of information, or that the process by which it gathers information is effective at demonstrating the helpfulness of these programs to students and their families. When the Department of Justice visits a school, it investigates whether the school has the required translators or interpreters on hand for communicating these requirements with parents. The process of engaging parents in meaningful ways may involve training and educating all members of the school's staff—particularly those involved with the intake of new students.

Remember that, if the parents opt out or waive these programs, according to ESSA and OCR, it remains the school's responsibility to ensure equal access to meet the student's English language needs to access educational programs, monitor the student's progress, and offer EL services again if a student is struggling. Opting out of or waiving services applies only to the receipt of direct ESL services. The school remains legally bound to provide appropriate English language development instruction in the general classroom setting.

To put a very fine point on it, opting or waiving out does not mean opting out of being classified as an EL. ESSA requires schools to provide this information in a manner that parents will understand.

DOJ and OCR Requirement 2: Providing Language Assistance

Federal Requirements:

All ELs are entitled to appropriate learning assistance services to become proficient in English and to participate equally in the standard instructional program within a reasonable time.

Schools can choose a program, provided it is educationally sound in theory.

The school can select its preferred language assistance program, including one of the following.

- **English as a second language pull-out or push-in embedded**: Students are pulled out for a period for this instruction (pull-out), or the ESL specialist comes into the classroom to co-teach with the general education teacher (push-in embedded).
- **Structured English immersion**: General education and ESL specialists are together all day, and the instruction is in English.
- **Sheltered English instruction**: ESL credentialed or certified teachers teach mathematics, science, language arts, or social studies in self-contained classrooms. This program is highly discouraged because in some districts students do not get credit for these subjects or receive rigorous standards-based instruction.
- **Bilingual or dual-language programs**: Teachers with bilingual credentials work with students in self-contained classrooms to learn concepts and core content in English and in a partner language.
- **Two-way immersion programs**: Typically, students are 50 percent English dominant and 50 percent dominant in another language; one bilingual certified teacher

teaches in the minority language 50 percent of the day, and the general education certified teacher teaches in English 50 percent of the day. Very few programs attain the 50–50 time frames. Some start with 10 percent time in English and 90 percent in the partner language; others use a 20–80 structure in kindergarten and shift to 50–50 around third or fourth grade.

The program you select must be educationally sound in theory and effective in application. There are many myths about these programs. One big myth is that it takes students seven or more years to become proficient in English. That premise is based on past ineffective instructional practices that lacked rigor and evidence (Thomas & Collier, 1997).

Chapters 2 and 3 (pages 29 and 51) describe in more detail the instructional components and classroom structures that schools can use to accelerate language, literacy, and content learning for ELs, regardless of the program schools choose. All other students benefit from greater academic gains as well. The program may not restrict the EL from participating in electives, enrichment, or advanced placement programs.

DOJ and OCR Requirement 3: Staffing and Supporting the EL Program

Federal Requirements:

ELs are entitled to programs with sufficient resources to ensure schools effectively implement them, including highly qualified teachers, support staff, and appropriate instructional materials.

Schools must have highly qualified teachers, staff, and administrators to effectively implement their EL program, and must provide supplemental training when necessary.

Massachusetts, Florida, and Arizona require all mainstream teachers to go through sheltered English instruction or ESL courses to work in the state. Massachusetts also requires all administrators to take fifteen hours of the administrators' version of the Rethinking Equity for Teaching English Language Learners course (RETELL), which additionally addresses how to observe and support sheltered English instruction teachers. In addition to this endorsement, all teachers and administrators must take an additional fifteen professional development hours to renew their license every five years. This ensures that ELs have qualified teachers in all grade levels. State licensure and education agencies whose relicensure requirements are lower than these should consider increasing to at least this minimum level to adequately comply with ESSA.

 Some states, districts, and schools offer extensive professional development, but not the follow-up expert coaching, peer coaching, and teacher learning communities that ensure transfer from training into the classroom where it can have a positive impact on ELs. Thus, EL achievement makes very little progress in those states.

 School structures must enable collaboration between ESL or ELD and content or general education teachers where they are encouraged to share practices, conduct peer coaching, and generate student support in all classrooms.

 Chapter 4 (page 65) concentrates on evidence-based professional development and follow-up systems that your school can adapt to experience accelerated student success.

DOJ and OCR Requirement 4: Providing Meaningful Access to All Curricular and Extracurricular Programs

Federal Requirements:

ELs must have access to grade-level curricula so that they can meet promotion and graduation requirements.

ELs are entitled to an equal opportunity to participate in all programs, including prekindergarten, magnet, gifted and talented, career and technical education, arts, and athletics programs; advanced placement and International Baccalaureate courses; clubs; and honors societies.

EL instruction must build language, literacy, and content simultaneously. ELs need to have access to STEM curricula and be college and career ready. Schools can accomplish this by providing teachers with a comprehensive continual professional development program that focuses on how to impart rigorous instruction to ELs. As we previously pointed out, this instruction must include all programs a school offers, be they supplemental, extracurricular, or advanced preparation.

There are multiple pathways to providing standards-based high-quality content instruction for ELs. Chapters 2, 3, and 4 (pages 29, 51, and 65) discuss these pathways.

Establish accountability measures with support systems for teachers and students. Develop, adapt, and adopt observation and evaluation systems reflecting the knowledge and special skills teachers need to effectively educate ELs within the context of other students. Chapters 4 and 5 (pages 65 and 85) elaborate on these evaluation systems.

DOJ and OCR Requirement 5: Avoiding Unnecessary Segregation

Federal Requirement:

ELs may not be segregated beyond those minutes where they receive ESL or an intervention necessary to help them succeed. They need to be part of the general education classroom(s) as much as possible.

ELs may be grouped together for ESL or sheltered English instruction classes to help them become more proficient in English while learning content. However, they need to participate with mainstream native English-speaking students the remainder of the day. They need English language role models, opportunities to integrate with other peers to feel part of the school, and access to the curricular and extracurricular benefits all other students have.

Special education ELs with severe disabilities may be in self-contained classrooms, but an ESL teacher must co-teach with the special education teacher.

Newcomers need special considerations. Some are highly schooled and need only English labels for concepts they already know. Those identified as SIFE need more time on instruction to learn English, core content concepts, and often the basics of attending school. For those students, well-designed after-school, Saturday, or summer-school programs help accelerate learning. Language interventions must be as diverse as the students' needs.

Segregating students for long periods of time also creates strained ethnic relations or antagonistic groups. Defuse potential tension between newcomers and long-term ELs or newcomers and other ethnic groups by including them in the general population as soon as possible. (See tips in chapters 3 and 4.)

DOJ and OCR Requirement 6: Evaluating ELs for Special Education and Providing Dual Services

Federal Requirements:

ELs with disabilities must receive both the language assistance and the disability-related services to which they are entitled under federal law.

To avoid inappropriately identifying ELs as students with disabilities because of their limited English proficiency, schools must evaluate ELs in an appropriate language based on the student's needs and skills.

It is important to include participants knowledgeable about that student's language needs in the team designing the plan.

Schools must evaluate ELs in English and in their primary language. Evaluating in all the primary languages can be a problem, since not all evaluators speak all languages and not all assessments are translated into every language. Sometimes it is difficult to find the appropriate assessments and evaluators even for common languages, such as Spanish. An LEA must show due diligence and make a reasonable attempt to assess each student as accurately and reliably as possible.

The school district bears ultimate responsibility for finding and hiring personnel and for maintaining the processes and tools for different language groups.

Special education services and English language instructional services are mutually required, and one does not supersede the other. Both amounts and types of services must conform to federal guidelines. Each set of services has specific requirements and thus mandates that an EL specialist be empaneled as a member of the student's individualized education program (IEP) development team.

DOJ and OCR Requirement 7: Meeting the Needs of Students Who Opt Out of EL Programs

Federal Requirements:

All ELs are entitled to services. Parents may, however, choose to remove their children from a school district's EL program or particular EL services within an EL program.

Schools may not recommend that parents opt out for any reason. Parents are entitled to guidance in a language with which they can understand their child's rights, the range of EL services their child can receive, and the benefits of such services. Schools should document that a parent made a voluntary, informed decision.

A school must provide services and access to educational programs to opted-out ELs; it must also monitor their progress and offer (appropriate) services again if the child is struggling.

Keeping meticulous data on opt-out ELs is critical. How well are they doing in mathematics, science, social studies, and language arts? What is their reading level? What about the syntax and academic language they exhibit in their writing? Do they need an intensive brief intervention in one of these areas?

Remember, parents' opting out of direct EL services does not absolve a school of providing English language development-based instruction to those students identified as ELs.

DOJ and OCR Requirement 8: Monitoring and Exiting ELs From EL Programs and Services

Federal Requirements:

School districts must monitor the progress of all EL students to ensure they achieve English language proficiency and acquire content knowledge within a reasonable period of time. Districts must annually administer a valid and reliable English language proficiency assessment—in reading, writing, listening, and speaking—that aligns with state English language proficiency standards.

An EL student must not exit EL programs, services, or status until he or she demonstrates English proficiency on an English language proficiency assessment in speaking, listening, reading, and writing.

School districts must monitor the academic progress of former EL students for at least two years to ensure that students have not prematurely exited; they have remedied any academic deficits they incurred from the EL program; and they are meaningfully participating in the district's educational programs comparable to their peers who were never EL students (never-EL peers).

Data collection for opt-outs should be included when monitoring former ELs as it is for all ELs.

Monitoring must also include processes in place to help exited formerly limited English proficient ELs with tutoring or interventions to prevent unforeseen gaps or focalization of their English language abilities.

DOJ and OCR Requirement 9: Evaluating the Effectiveness of the Program

Federal Requirements:

EL programs must be reasonably calculated to enable EL students to attain English proficiency and meaningful participation in the standard educational program comparable to their never-EL peers.

School districts must monitor and compare over time the academic performance of EL students in the program and those who exited the program relative to that of their never-EL peers.

School districts must evaluate EL programs over time using accurate data to assess the educational performance of current and former EL students in a comprehensive and reliable way and must modify their programs when needed.

Identifying implementation data is part of the initial professional development where all teachers and administrators participate and set goals and milestones to evaluate the program and whole-school involvement.

Triangulate EL data on learning progressions on state tests such as the ACCESS, with report cards from core content classrooms, with professional development effectiveness data and implementation data.

Schoolwide implementation, evaluation, and support of professional development targeted at academic language strategies, modeling, and practice in all subject areas is a must to ensure that all students have the skills to meet the rigorous academic state standards for career and college readiness.

DOJ and OCR Requirement 10: Ensuring Meaningful Communication With EL Parents

Federal Requirement:

EL parents are entitled to meaningful communication in a language they understand, such as through translated materials or a language interpreter, and to adequate notice of information of any school program, service, or activity.

Teachers can use many of the vocabulary and reading strategies we describe in chapter 2 (page 38–41) to attract and engage EL parents.

The school district is ultimately responsible for hiring and having available translators and translated forms in various languages. This system must include a nonwritten form of communication, as some parents of ELs may not be able to read in their primary language. Messaging and communicating to all stakeholders is covered in chapter 6 (page 99).

Visit www2.ed.gov/about/offices/list/ocr/ellresources.html for more information about school districts' obligations to English learner students and limited English proficient parents. Use figure 1.1 (page 26) to gauge your challenges, progress, and evidence of compliance against the ten key federal requirements.

Requirement	Current Challenges	In Progress: Evidence	In Place: Evidence
1. Identifying and assessing students			
2. Providing language assistance			
3. Staffing and supporting the EL program			
4. Providing meaningful access to all curricular and extracurricular programs			
5. Avoiding unnecessary segregation			
6. Evaluating ELs for special education and providing dual services			
7. Meeting the needs of students who opt out of EL programs			
8. Monitoring and exiting ELs from EL programs and services			
9. Evaluating the effectiveness of the program			
10. Ensuring meaningful communication with EL parents			

Figure 1.1: Gauging implementation and compliance.

*Visit **go.SolutionTree.com/EL** for a free reproducible version of this figure.*

Where to Obtain Funding

Good news—ESSA gives more flexibility to states and local educational agencies on how to allocate Title I funds to support schools with more ELs. ESSA's flexibility and expanded definitions ensure that more teachers, of all grade levels and subject areas, are eligible to receive federal Title I funds, which support disadvantaged students, and Title II funds, which support professional development for teachers and administrators. However, school leaders and advocacy groups need to be well versed on the provisions of ESSA. Schools should consult their districts or state education agencies to inquire about such funding. They must also be vigilant and advocate for support and clarity to ensure that the students most in need receive priority for services. Title III will continue to fund special language programs.

Many ELs might also qualify for services under Title I, part C, Education of Migratory Children; part E, Family Engagement in Education Programs; Title VII, Impact Aid; and Title IX, Education for the Homeless and Others. Schools should also consult their state education agencies for information on these funding possibilities. Staff that work with ELs and other targeted populations may receive professional development support under the same titles and sections as the students. But they will also have access to Title II, Preparing, Training, and Recruiting High-Quality Teachers, Principals, and Other School Leaders.

Conclusion

Schools, school districts, and states can comply with federal laws as they analyze which of the *Dear Colleague Letter* guidelines they are meeting and which need to be addressed. This chapter provides firsthand information about how Massachusetts was able to come into compliance with their services as well as the details on the ten key federal guidelines. Chapter 2 describes the type of instructional components that are acceptable under federal requirements.

Discussion Questions

Consider the following.

- How many Be on the Lookout items from the ten Department of Justice requirements do we currently have in place? How many are in progress? How do we know?
- Who do we need to include in this process? What human capital and resources do we already have in place to help facilitate whole-school implementation of compliant service to our ELs?

CHAPTER 2

Instructional Components and Strategies for Teaching ELs

Strategy

Academic definition: A careful plan or method for achieving a particular goal usually over a long period of time

Friendly definition: A way to get something done

There are three basic instructional building blocks that can help ELs and all other students achieve at higher academic levels when all content and ESL teachers integrate them into their daily teaching repertoire: (1) academic vocabulary and discourse, (2) reading comprehension, and (3) writing skills. This chapter maps out the research behind this type of instruction. We describe the twelve components for achieving language mastery, reading comprehension and writing skills development; how to plan lessons; and how to teach all components in an integrated fashion. At the end of the chapter, we offer suggested time frames, the content for designing professional development, and the expected outcomes for teachers and students when these components are implemented with fidelity.

There is extensive research and evidence behind these instructional components. The Carnegie Corporation panel on adolescent literacy for language minority students (Short & Fitzsimmons, 2007) found that English learners have double the work in schools because they have to learn English *and* master the content that all other students are required to learn. Although ESL teachers spend thirty or so minutes a day with ELs, the reality is that most ELs spend the majority of the day with mainstream content teachers. This is not effective support of EL students. The panel identified a dire need for professional development that assists both ESL and ELD teachers and mainstream content teachers in integrating vocabulary, reading comprehension, and writing skills into their lessons and daily instruction. As we discuss throughout the rest of this chapter, the existing instructional and professional development models used in the past need to delve deeper and be more rigorous than existing sheltered English instruction models.

The Development of ExC-ELL

To address the need for a comprehensive professional development program for general education, ESL and ELD, and bilingual teachers, the Carnegie Corporation of New York funded a five-year study (Calderón, 2009a). This study resulted in a professional development model called Expediting Comprehension for English Language Learners (ExC-ELL), which derives from previous five-year studies funded by the U.S. Department of Education, U.S. Department of Labor, National Institute of Child Health and Human Development, and the Texas Education Agency. ExC-ELL, which features twelve components that are the basis of this book, was tested in low-performing schools in New York City and Hawaii. It resulted in those schools becoming exemplary schools in just two years (Calderón, 2009a). The twelve components begin with vocabulary instruction as a precursor to reading and writing, hence, the instructional sequence for both ExC-ELL and RETELL is as follows.

The Twelve ExC-ELL Components

1. Preteach key vocabulary words and phrases before reading.

2. Conduct teacher think-alouds to model the reading comprehension strategy.

3. Students conduct paired reading or triad reading when working with a newcomer.

4. Students conduct partner summarization, and teacher monitors use of new vocabulary.

5. Conduct depth of word study and grammar minilessons from the reading text.

6. Lead class debriefings and discussions to help students hear and practice more words and discourse.

7. Use cooperative learning strategies to provide opportunities for higher-order discourse to develop.

8. Allow students to formulate questions instead of always answering questions.

9. Conduct Roundtable Reviews, which help students review all the words they have learned.

10. Conduct prewriting and drafting for text-based writing in teams of three or four.

11. Teach a variety of revising and editing strategies.

12. Asses final product and performance based on criteria established at the beginning of the project.

As of this writing, schools and districts in Virginia, North Carolina, and Texas, as well as the cities of Memphis and New York, have implemented ExC-ELL and have seen great results with their ELs as well as all other students. Schools in New York City, Salt Lake City, and Kauai moved from low-performing to high-performing schools. Chapters 4 and 5 elaborate on what these new sites implemented that created success (see also Calderón, 2007a, 2009a, 2009b, 2011b).

When the Massachusetts Department of Elementary and Secondary Education recognized the importance of training general education teachers through a sheltered English instruction model they used the twelve ExC-ELL components to develop their program for training teachers and administrators. The state requires up to forty-five hours of professional development for all teachers and fifteen hours for all administrators in the state. It is expected that schools in the state of Massachusetts will improve in 2016 after the training of the forty thousand educators is complete. We describe the content of that professional development at the end of this chapter.

What Research Recommends for the Content of Schoolwide Professional Development

There is a strong consensus about the importance of explicitly teaching vocabulary before teaching reading comprehension and writing to ELs at all grade levels and in all subject areas because depth and breadth of vocabulary correlate with increased reading proficiency and understanding (Kamil & Hiebert, 2005). Lesson delivery components must include strategies to explicitly select and teach words that will pose challenges and stimulate ELs before, during, and after reading (Beck et al., 2002; Calderón et al., 2005; Calderón, 2007a; Carlo, August, & Snow, 2005). We call this process of fostering word consciousness *semantic awareness* (Graves, 2006). School principals of ExC-ELL schools call it *semantic atmosphere in the school* (Calderón, 2007a). Regardless of terminology, it is a process that accelerates word learning and reading comprehension in EL students.

ELs need decoding and fluency practice in order to become good readers—to simultaneously recognize words and comprehend a text (Samuels, 2002). Sometimes ELs receive too much instruction on decoding and not enough on comprehension. Phonics-only programs do not work with ELs (Kamil & Hiebert, 2005). The better the foundation ELs have in word recognition, along with word meaning, the more focus they can give to overall meaning, which builds both comprehension and fluency.

Achieving this goal requires *strategic processing of text*, which means that teachers know how to develop cognitive and metacognitive strategies necessary for text comprehension of mathematics, science, and social studies texts. Instructional strategies include direct instruction, teacher modeling, and opportunities for partner and team practice of skills (Deshler, Palincsar, Biancarosa, & Nair, 2007). Techniques that enhance comprehension include self-monitoring for understanding; using semantic, graphic, or conceptual organizers; answering questions and obtaining immediate feedback; formulating questions about the text and obtaining immediate feedback; becoming aware of the genre characteristics and text structure; summarizing key points; summarizing the content; and retelling a story or a process. Core comprehension strategies for the different text structures include predicting, determining important information, summarizing, making inferences, visualizing, asking and answering questions, monitoring comprehension, and making connections (August et al., 2008; August & Shanahan, 2006; Kamil & Hiebert, 2005; National Reading Panel, 2000; Snow, 2002).

Anchoring language, literacy, and content knowledge includes cooperative learning strategies that provide ample opportunities for student interaction. Cooperative learning strategies set a safe context for language practice for ELs (Calderón, Hertz-Lazarowitz, & Slavin, 1998; McGroarty & Calderón, 2005). Management of student interaction with peers helps students gain a deeper understanding of word meanings, infer across content area lessons, and apply higher-order thinking skills. Teachers use interaction strategies to consolidate knowledge of a lesson, unit, or instructional event.

ELs need modeling of every type of writing. They need to learn a variety of writing text types within each content area (for example, argumentative, informative and expository, and narrative) and text structures (for example, problem and solution, cause and effect, descriptive, sequential, and compare and contrast). ELs, like most students, also need practice with language mechanics, revising strategies, and editing strategies. They need to develop literacy skills for each content area as they simultaneously learn, comprehend, and apply content-area concepts in English.

Features of Effective Instruction for ELs in Content Classrooms

Lesson plans across all subjects need to reflect the twelve ExC-ELL components, using a cyclical vocabulary, reading, and writing approach that continues to teach or highlight both comprehension and fluency throughout the cycle. The first step is to plan a lesson reflecting that cycle. Teachers use the twelve basic components of the cycle for teaching a lesson. We cover both the planning and the delivery of a lesson in this section.

Planning the Lessons

Planning cyclical lessons for ELs involves seven basic steps that you should guide your teachers in implementing in their content area. The professional development that you offer for the whole school staff, after they have been presented with the twelve components, should also include how to plan the lessons. Teachers can work with their own textbooks and texts at the end of each day of training in order to incorporate all the basic elements of a lesson. The following seven steps guide the lesson planning.

1. **Parse the selected texts.** The teacher preselects a text and parses the text, breaking it up into sections that students can work with effectively in a class period. From each section, the teacher selects five words or phrases to teach before reading (spending two minutes per word).

2. **Integrate core content standards.** The text should reflect a content standard that teachers can write in the lesson template.

3. **Integrate language standards.** Many states require teachers to post a language objective along with the content objective in the lesson template. This helps hold ELs and all students accountable for using those five words or phrases in their discussions and writing.

4. **Select vocabulary tiers one, two, and three.** Teachers choose the five words to teach from the tier one, tier two, and tier three categories. These categories are different from Beck et al. because they have been developed for EL instruction (Calderón et al., 2005). The five words are for all students to master, including ELs at different proficiency levels. Newcomers might need some additional words, but if they are in the class, teachers must also hold them accountable for using the five words as they participate in the teaching and learning events.

5. **Select classroom management and grouping.** Questions to consider: Should we use teams of four or three? Pairs for some activities? Teams in stations? What social norms or reminders do students need for each grouping? The teams should be heterogeneous by race, gender, and English proficiency levels.

6. **Select interaction activities.** Questions to consider: Should teachers use a whole-class activity for review such as Shoe Buddies, Clock Buddies, or Corners, where students get out of their desks and meet with a different peer to summarize or practice a skill? A Numbered Heads

Together (described later in this chapter and in chapter 6, page 111) after students formulate questions? Some other get-up-and-summarize activity? What social norms or reminders do students need for each grouping?

7. **Select ancillary materials.** Questions to consider: Do I need table tents with lists of tier two words? Which transition words do I highlight? Colored paper for foldables where the students keep track of the new words? Markers? Scissors? Index cards?

Tier One, Tier Two, and Tier Three

Tier one: Basic words ELs need to communicate, read, and write. These are simple words (*blender*, *tooth*, and *toothache*) that any second-grade monolingual English student knows but a newcomer EL entering at whatever level would not necessarily know.

Tier two: Information-processing words that nest the subject-specific tier-three words in long sentences, polysemous words (*body*, *trunk*, *left*), transition words, connectors—more sophisticated words for rich discussions and specificity in descriptions (*moreover*, *as a result*, *nevertheless*, *initially*).

Tier three: Subject-specific words that label discipline concepts, subjects, and topics; infrequently used academic words (*photosynthesis*, *foreshadow*, *legion*).

Once the lesson is mapped out, review the sequence of activities and instructional strategies along with the time frames the teacher will have to teach the lesson. Literacy coaches, leaders, and administrators should also review these lessons and offer feedback. ESL and core content teachers can jointly plan lessons that are appropriate for ELs at different levels of proficiency for the ESL teacher to co-teach.

Integrating the Twelve Components of a Comprehensive Lesson

As a leader dedicated to supporting ELs, it's imperative that your teachers understand how to integrate the twelve components into a comprehensive lesson. In addition to the lesson template, you can also use a classroom observation protocol to plan the lesson.

Here is an example of how you can apply the twelve steps to your lesson plan.

1. **Preteach five vocabulary words** and phrases before reading. More words can be taught during and after reading.

2. **Conduct teacher think-alouds** to model the comprehension strategy for the standard—for example, finding evidence, determining cause and effect, looking for context clues, and uncovering unfamiliar words.

3. **Conduct paired or partner reading and triad reading** with a newcomer for the first parsed section. Partners read together, alternating sentences and summarizing after each paragraph.

4. **Monitor** vocabulary application, partner reading, and partner summarization while students are practicing with their partners. Record some examples of discourse for each student and newcomers. This is important because newcomers need to learn more to catch up with their EL and mainstream peers, and these samples of their discourse let teachers know how much they are progressing in their English proficiency.

5. **Conduct depth of word study and grammar minilessons** from the reading text. Point out certain sentence structures you want to see in students' writing, such as prefixes, suffixes, and so on.

6. **Lead class debriefings and discussions** to help students hear and practice more words and discourse.

7. **Use cooperative learning strategies** to provide opportunities for higher-order discourse to develop.

8. **Have students formulate questions** instead of always answering questions. Students go back into the text, reread deliberately, and ponder word meanings in order to formulate questions that will be shared with the whole class.

9. **Conduct Roundtable Reviews**, which help students review all the words they have learned in the cycle before they begin the formal writing process. Students take a few

minutes to compete and write as many vocabulary words from the reading as they can remember.

10. **Conduct prewriting and drafting** for text-based writing at first in teams of three or four. This creates synergy and a more thoughtful and thorough first draft.

11. **Students revise and edit** during team writing, work with a writing partner to practice and perfect their work, and eventually to progress to individual writing.

12. **Assess final product and performance** based on criteria established at the beginning of the project. Assessments can come in a variety of forms such as essays, team products, formal presentations, and multimedia. Performance assessments such as checklists or note taking during interaction with peers gives teachers better information than vocabulary tests or the textbook questions. The ultimate proof of learning is in the students' writing.

Building the Process

If preK–12 teachers instruct ELs in five words or phrases per subject per day, that amounts to twenty-five words a day. Imagine the possibilities for a week and for the whole school year. It amounts to three thousand to five thousand words each year. Extensive explicit vocabulary instruction becomes the basis of EL success in all schools. In our observational studies we found that higher test scores for ELs and striving readers were the result of students having larger vocabularies and deeper comprehension. Without understanding 80–90 percent of the words in sentences or tests, a student cannot grasp the concepts to be learned, respond to questions, or enjoy reading. Furthermore, without specific academic vocabulary, ELs cannot keep up with their subject classes. Non-EL students also benefit from this focus on vocabulary. Otherwise, they become struggling readers because their word knowledge is limited.

Teachers report that teaching a rich vocabulary, along with reading integrated into math, science, and social studies, helps all students perform better in class discussions, writing, and tests. Whether gifted or just learning English as an additional language, all students need explicit and varied instruction to build solid word power. Essentially, teaching vocabulary should be pervasive throughout the school. The more teachers are involved in systematic vocabulary instruction, the faster ELs, striving students and struggling readers, and students with special education services learn and succeed.

With this baseline knowledge for how to best design a lesson plan and its needed components firmly in mind, let's look at how you can help teachers adapt this methodology specifically to the teaching of vocabulary, reading, and writing.

How to Teach Vocabulary to English Learners and All Readers

Per the first step in the twelve components of a comprehensive lesson, educators should teach five words for each subject each day and spend no more than two to three minutes on each. This explicit vocabulary instruction for ELs has developed into a seven-step process, called 7 Steps. Educators can teach this process to the whole class, or in small groups, using PowerPoint presentations and interactive whiteboards or even large chart paper.

- **Step 1:** Teacher says and shows the word and asks students to repeat it three times.
- **Step 2:** Teacher reads and shows the word in a sentence (context) from the text students will be reading.
- **Step 3:** Teacher provides the definitions from the glossary or dictionary.
- **Step 4:** Teacher explains meaning with student-friendly definitions or gives an example that students can relate to.
- **Step 5:** Teacher highlights an aspect of the word that might create difficulty: spelling, multiple meanings, cognates and false cognates, prefixes, suffixes, base words, synonyms, antonyms, homophones, grammatical variations, and so on.
- **Step 6:** Teacher engages 100 percent of the students in ways to orally use the word and concept. (For example, students turn to their partner and use the word in a complete sentence, share back and forth, about five examples each.) The teacher provides a sentence frame or sentence starter containing the target vocabulary word or phrase to help learners.

- **Step 7:** The teacher reminds students that they will be accountable. They have to use the word or phrase later on as they read and stop to verbally summarize with a peer or in an exit ticket or writing assignment.

Table 2.1 includes a simple list of dos and don'ts educators should keep firmly in mind when teaching vocabulary.

Table 2.1: Dos and Don'ts for Teaching Vocabulary

Do	Don't
Have students produce the words orally at least five times each with peers in meaningful sentences.	Ask students to look up the word in the dictionary. It takes too much time, and they usually pick the wrong meaning.
Ensure even beginning proficiency students can learn and use the five pretaught vocabulary words when provided with sentence frames.	Ask students to copy definition or sentences from the board as you are preteaching vocabulary.
Teach key tier one, two, and three words before reading, not after. More words can be taught after reading and before writing.	Ask students to draw pictures during the preteaching of vocabulary.
Spend only two or three minutes preteaching a word or phrase (one minute for teacher's steps 1–5 and 7; one minute for students' step 6).	Spend more than ten to twelve minutes preteaching five key vocabulary words or phrases.
Have students use the five pretaught words in their oral summaries during partner reading.	Let any EL or newcomer pass or remain silent during step 6. He or she can participate with sentence frames.
Provide the cognate or translated word, or ask a peer to do so, should a newcomer need a translation. However, the newcomer must be accountable for using the word in English throughout the lesson. They can repeat what their partner says if needed.	Ask peers to translate for newcomers without also teaching them the word or phrase or complete sentence in English. Peers and newcomers should be accountable for also learning five words per subject per day.

How to Teach Reading to English Learners and All Readers

English learners need to read, discuss, and start some writing to anchor the new words. For ELs in the beginning stages, the text should be broken into small segments. This way, they are reading something different every day but are engaged in greater analysis and application as they learn and apply new vocabulary, grammar, and writing. Repetitive reading of the same long passages does not help ELs develop fluency or comprehension because ELs focus on reading quickly and not on comprehension. Silent reading does not help either; it becomes pretend reading. It also creates bad habits in students. They begin to think that skimming and looking at pictures is reading. We recommend that teachers use the following sequence of steps to teach reading to their students.

1. **Teacher models strategic reading in each content area.** Mathematics, science, social studies, and language arts teachers can conduct think-alouds with a short passage for about three to four minutes to model strategic reading. They can model reading comprehension strategies such as determining important information, summarizing, making inferences, visualizing, asking and answering questions, making connections, and monitoring comprehension.

2. **Student reads and summarizes.** Immediately after the teacher models, partners should begin reading alternating sentences, followed by summarizing after each paragraph and applying the think-aloud strategy the teacher asked them to use. ELs need to hear themselves and others read for fluency and pronunciation. Partner summaries give ELs opportunities to practice their new language in safe contexts with peers. Partner reading can take about ten to twelve minutes. In elementary schools, the teacher reads a section as students follow along by tracking what the teacher reads. The teacher stops after brief intervals to ask students to summarize with their partners using as many words from the pretaught vocabulary and from the text as possible. When students go to stations to read independently, the teacher also instructs them to stop at certain intervals and summarize with their partners.

3. **Student engages in after-reading activities to anchor knowledge, reading comprehension, and language.** All students need to practice close reading. Hence, after they have read a sizable portion of a text with their partners,

the teacher should conduct a minilesson on how to formulate questions. The Bloom's taxonomy charts give students question starters for each level of the taxonomy (www.nwlink.com/~donclark/hrd/bloom.html) and serve as a great tool for question formulation. Each team of four should generate two questions and answers. The teacher can collect these, check them for accuracy, and use them to test the students with cooperative learning strategies such as Numbered Heads Together (see Calderón et al., 2016, for descriptions of these and other after-reading activities).

For students with interrupted formal educations and ELs with special education needs, teachers can also teach decoding and phonemic awareness in the context of presenting vocabulary. These students, who require intensive reading intervention, benefit from additional time on reading specifically using a developed program such as the Reading Instructional Goals for Older Readers (RIGOR) (Calderon, 2007b). This program is a curriculum that has day-by-day lessons for ESL, special education, or reading teachers. It follows the ExC-ELL sequence and instructional methodology for teaching reading but adds phonological awareness activities and more vocabulary. These lessons integrate phonics with vocabulary and reading comprehension skills through leveled books about science and social studies.

How to Teach Writing to Anchor Language, Literacy, and Content

The final piece in the sequence of instruction is students writing about what they are learning. Teachers can introduce daily small pieces of writing related to what ELs are reading, with one summative piece each week. EL students understand and learn grammatical and syntactical features, such as prepositional phrases, spelling, tense, compound sentences, and passive voice, faster when the teacher points out these features in the text students are reading. Writing in science is different from writing in social studies or formulating mathematical questions. All content writing is different from the writing process most students are exposed to in language arts. As in vocabulary and reading instruction, the teacher must model the desired outcome and then have students practice. Have your teachers provide this instruction using the following steps and then have them conduct performance assessments for students in teams of three or four, gradually moving to individual assessments (Calderón, 2011a, 2011b).

1. **Preteach the most important vocabulary.** Select key words that students will need to understand and use for writing assignments and grading.

2. **Use a mentor text for reading before writing.** Reading a text gives students the content and sample sentence structures to use in their writing. Develop background knowledge or explanations of unfamiliar concepts and mechanics for writing.

3. **Present the text structure to use.** Discuss and present the structure (e.g., argumentative, descriptive, narrative), its purpose, benefits, and goals, and the grading rules of finished products.

4. **Model it.** Model each phase of the writing process (e.g., drafting in teams, revising, editing, final product).

5. **Memorize it.** Ensure that students memorize the language and steps of the strategy.

6. **Support it.** Support or scaffold the EL's use of the strategy until he or she can apply it with little or no support. Model self-regulated learning and the use of mnemonic devices.

7. **Ample Use of Student Interaction.** Model and implement collaborative and cooperative writing strategies to plan, draft, revise, and edit compositions.

8. **Differentiated Assessment.** Consider differentiated grading scales for ELs, depending on their level of English proficiency. Assess the point of entry for writing and continue measuring the learning progression of writing since the oral, reading and writing proficiencies for ELs vary dramatically. Newcomers to the country may have good writing skills in the primary language but what constitutes good writing there may be different from our expectations. A student who has been in U.S. schools since kindergarten may have oral fluency but no literacy skills in either the first or second language. (Calderón, 2011b)

Helping your educators establish and effectively use vocabulary, reading, and writing lesson plans using these guidelines requires an investment of time and energy in their professional development. The next section provides you with the information you need to organize and set up a process for that development.

How to Organize a Professional Development Program for the Twelve Instructional Components

The first step in establishing an effective professional development program for supporting ELs is to have all the teachers and administrators in the school read about teaching vocabulary prior to the professional development on that topic (see appendix A, page 125). After attending the professional development session on vocabulary, expert coaches who are familiar with the instruction outlined in this chapter should visit classrooms, using an implementation protocol to help build teacher confidence and fine-tune their instructional practices. Simultaneously, teachers are sharing, problem solving, and analyzing student progress in their teams. Subsequently, everyone should read the teaching reading content in this chapter, as well as the professional development content in chapter 4, and the coaching and team learning community content in chapter 5. Apply this same sequence to teaching writing.

Expected Outcomes With Each Focus of Professional Development

In establishing effective teaching strategies to support your EL students, we recommend breaking up your professional development into five separate steps, each of which involves six hours of focused professional development. Each step comes with specific intended outcomes for students, teachers, coaches, and administrators alike. After going through each stage of professional development, teachers and administrators can come back to these descriptions and reflect on what they learned and what each teacher needs for proper implementation. Administrators should discuss how they will support the teachers and their role as implementation leaders. These steps begin with the expected outcomes for the students, followed by the expectations for teachers, coaches, and administrators to adhere to in order to ensure the necessary student outcomes.

Step 1: Six Hours of Professional Development on Vocabulary Instruction

- **Outcomes for students:** Students must learn vocabulary words from different categories that their teachers select from the texts they are about to read; they learn more vocabulary on the run as they read and discuss with peers; they learn additional words as they delve into depth-of-word-knowledge activities and apply new words to different types of writing—summaries, reports, and creative writing, to name a few.

- **Training for teachers:** With trainers modeling each segment, kindergarten to twelfth-grade teachers practice how to select words to teach according to their students' language and reading levels. The tier one, two, and three words range from easy to sophisticated to content-specific words, concept-laden words, and words that nest those concepts. Teachers learn how to explicitly preteach vocabulary and orchestrate practice and mastery through discourse protocols and word analysis activities during and after reading. Teachers also practice syntactic processing so they can teach students how grammar knowledge supports reading comprehension. They bring sample student products to the next training session to discuss successes and problems.

- **Training for coaches and administrators:** Coaches and administrators learn how to observe vocabulary instructional delivery and how students apply new words. They learn to use a valid and reliable observation protocol designed specifically to record EL performance and teacher performance on vocabulary and discourse, as well as how to give effective feedback on depth and breadth of teachers' and students' word usage.

Step 2: Six Hours of Professional Development on Reading Instruction

- **Outcomes for students:** Students learn and apply reading strategies that support comprehension and subject domain mastery.

- **Training for teachers:** With trainers modeling each segment, kindergarten to second-grade teachers practice with peers how to teach fluency and comprehension together. Using think-alouds, trainers model, effective reading comprehension strategies (for example, using text features, using text structures, summarizing, forming questions, and monitoring comprehension), purposes for reading, and learning from reading. Kindergarten to twelfth-grade teachers learn to integrate relevant strategies within the text students are about to read. Teachers also learn cooperative learning strategies that support discussions of text with particular verbal strategies (for example, for recall, paraphrasing, summarization, question formulation, and sentence-starter frames). SIFE and ESL teachers learn how to combine phonemic awareness, phonological awareness, decoding, word knowledge, fluency, and comprehension of content texts. All teachers learn how to set up student pairs for paired reading and how to monitor for quality reading and application of comprehension strategies. Teachers also participate in teams of four to experience firsthand the management strategies that create effective cooperative contexts for learning. Teachers bring observation notes on the use of these strategies by their ELs and other students.

- **Training for coaches and administrators:** By recording student responses on the observation protocol during teacher read-alouds, student-partner reading, peer discussions, and cooperative learning activities, coaches and administrators can give specific feedback to teachers and students on the application of reading comprehension strategies. Coaches and administrators bring sample anonymous observation protocols for discussion and feedback on their observations to their own professional development sessions.

Step 3: Six Hours of Professional Development on Writing Instruction

- **Outcomes for students:** Students focus on text structures and writing conventions to compose a variety of texts that demonstrate clear focus, logical development of ideas in well-organized paragraphs, awareness of the audience, and use of appropriate language to advance the author's purpose for writing across the curriculum.

- **Training for teachers:** Trainers model the development of literary, expository or procedural, or persuasive texts or research. *Literary* includes stories, poems, personal narratives, scripts, and literary responses. *Expository or procedural* includes informational text, letters, analytical essays, and multimedia presentations. *Persuasive texts* include persuasive essays and argumentative essays. Teachers practice highlighting and presenting features of various types of text structures with their own textbooks. They also learn to integrate writing strategies (for example, identifying main ideas and author's purpose and connecting various parts of a text), editing activities and strategies (for example, rewriting sentences, eliminating unnecessary repetition, spelling, and grammar), and effective use of writing tools (for example, table tents, outlines, concept maps, semantic maps, and graphic organizers) as they relate to different disciplines.

- **Training for coaches and administrators:** Coaches and administrators learn how to record on the observation protocol the complexities of teaching writing mechanics and processes in order to give precise feedback to teachers. Administrators also learn how to conduct constructive and robust teacher evaluations that continually inform and improve teaching for ELs and other students.

What Does Productive Teaching and Learning Look Like in EL Classrooms?

- ELs learn five new words per subject through oral practice with step 6 of the 7 Steps and the teacher holds them accountable for using those words during the lesson. They learn twenty-five words a day but learn more in the process of reading and summarizing.

- ELs respond in short sentences, phrases, or single words, but they participate in all core content classroom discussions.

- ELs read every day through shadow reading, choral reading, or partner reading. They do individual silent reading at home.

- ELs write in exit tickets what they have learned.

- ELs receive specific instructional interventions when necessary.

- ELs are assessed in all subject areas with performance assessment measures to ensure systematic improvement.

Step 4: Six Hours of Professional Development on Higher-Order Thinking Skills and Performance Assessment

- **Outcomes for students:** Students practice what they learned previously and learn the intricacies of academic oral discourse, communication skills, social and cooperative skills, self-evaluation, and creativity.

- **Training for teachers:** Teachers learn how to develop additional skills for ELs—and all students (for example, critical thinking, collaboration, communication, technology, problem solving, life and career skills such as flexibility and adaptability, initiative and self-direction, social and cross-cultural productivity and accountability, leadership, and responsibility). Teachers use props and activities to help students practice effective communication (for example, sentence and question starters; social protocols; instructions on how to interrupt politely, question, and reach consensus). Teachers learn myriad cooperative learning structures and technology for different learning purposes. Teachers practice relinquishing control and empower students to become more creative in their learning and in the products or performances of that learning, and practice self-regulation and evaluation.

Teachers learn to assess EL learning through performance and portfolio assessment and through other differentiated testing techniques. They further their reflection through observation protocols to determine whether their teaching is reaching all students.

- **Training for coaches and administrators:** Coaches and administrators learn to record effective discourse and interactional patterns that facilitate language learning, content concepts, and 21st century skills.

Step 5: Six Hours on Teacher Learning Communities for Gauging Learning Progressions of ELs, Teachers, Coaches, and Administrators

For the fifth step of the professional development, all educators learn how to sustain the learning from the previous days. Chapter 5 elaborates on tools for keeping track of everyone's learning. It also makes suggestions for coaching and evaluation. Teachers can learn from professional development institutes or workshops five days in a row or one day at a time. Either way, expert coaches need to help the teachers during their first trials in their classrooms.

Conclusion

The twelve components of ExC-ELL have been developed and tested to work with the diversity of ELs as well as the non-ELs who share the core content classrooms with them. It is critically important that the instructional strategies described for teaching vocabulary, reading, and writing be integrated into all content areas as well as in the ESL instruction. The framework for the professional development model we outlined in this chapter was designed to include all core content and ESL teachers. In addition to the language, literacy, and content integration, the social-emotional being of your students can also be integrated in this model. Chapter 3 is devoted to social-emotional learning, which entails adding one or two more days of professional development in order to integrate seamlessly into the teachers' daily lessons. Chapters 5, 6, and 7 delve deeper into the professional development design and the follow-up coaching and teacher support systems that ensure transfer from the training into the teachers' instructional repertoire and the students' learning.

Discussion Questions

Consider the following.

For all schools:

- Do learners other than ELs need to develop and apply academic vocabulary?

For elementary schools:

- Does the instruction in all grade levels teach three thousand to five thousand words a year? If not, how can this change? If so, how do you know?
- Are a high percentage of students reading at grade level by first grade? If not, what is the cause? What type of professional development for teachers and special intervention for students can you design?
- What type of professional development for teachers and what type of special intervention is necessary for SIFE?
- How many LT-ELs will the fifth grade be sending to middle school? What intensive intervention can you implement right away?

For secondary schools:

- Do all subject-area teachers teach five words per subject per day?
- What type of professional development for teachers and what type of special intervention is necessary for SIFE?
- How many LT-ELs will the eighth grade be sending to high school? What intensive intervention can you implement right away?

CHAPTER 3

English Language Development and Social and Emotional Skills

By Hector Montenegro, Ed. D.

Empathy

Academic definition: Empathy is the ability to accurately identify the emotional states of others and respond to them with care and concern

Friendly definition: Seeing with the eyes of another, listening with the ears of another, and feeling with the heart of another —*Alfred Adler*

EL students entering a new school environment can find it intimidating, challenging, and even frightening. They are entering another world where they don't understand the language, the culture differs from what they are used to, and rules and the academic expectations of the school often appear unrealistic and unattainable. In effect, they are "caught between two worlds" (Igoa, 1995, p. 85). In addition to making sure that ELs become proficient in English by focusing on academic language in all content areas, teachers have the responsibility of creating a classroom environment that is inclusive and safe for all students to learn, and where students feel supported socially and emotionally.

To help ELs transition into the new environment with less stress and anxiety, teachers can facilitate the learning of social and emotional skills, model social and emotional learning competencies, and provide students ample opportunities to reinforce these competencies through highly engaging instructional strategies. The research is conclusive—explicit instruction of social and emotional skills and competencies enables students to have greater academic gains, positive feelings about school and adults in school, fewer disciplinary problems, and less stress and anxiety (Durlak, Weissberg, Dymnicki, Taylor, & Schellinger, 2011). This is why basic activities, such as making ELs feel welcome in the school and classroom, incorporating their language and culture into the instructional framework, and facilitating peer-to-peer interaction and cooperation in an academic setting, are essential to ensuring EL success. In a learning environment where students can thrive socially and emotionally, and where there is greater peer modeling of language, ELs will have more academic success. Secondary benefits to such a positive and interactive learning environment include increasing empathy on the part of English-dominant peers, which makes it safe for ELs to experiment with language without being teased, humiliated, and bullied. Teachers, however, can't do it alone. School administrators must support, model, and facilitate the full integration of social and emotional skills with literacy strategies and academic content in order to ensure consistency of implementation that is sustained over time.

Social and Emotional Learning

Social and emotional learning involves processes through which children and adults develop fundamental emotional and social competencies to understand and manage emotions, set and achieve positive goals, feel and show empathy for others, establish and maintain positive relationships, and make responsible decisions (Collaborative for Academic, Social, and Emotional Learning [CASEL], 2013).

Implementing social and emotional learning in the school is in the best interest of all students and adults. English learners often come to school without the social skills necessary to navigate the new language and cultural norms and respond in socially correct ways. This lack of familiarity and awkwardness with the new culture impacts the self-concept and confidence of ELs. Acquiring a new language is in itself a social and emotional process. However, in a school where social and emotional learning is fully implemented, classroom environments tend to be more inclusive, positive, and encouraging while fostering respect and valuing diversity.

Teachers who demonstrate social and emotional learning competencies intentionally facilitate interaction and cooperation among students of all backgrounds and proficiency levels; create classrooms in which students feel safe and free to take risks without fear of being ridiculed, teased, or ostracized; and encourage students in every way. Such a school is full of praise, compliments, and constructive feedback that serve to motivate and guide students to accelerate their academic achievement and social integration (CASEL, 2013). However, a strong social and emotional learning program is still not enough for ELs unless schools integrate it with the appropriate academic English language acquisition and core content knowledge they need to graduate college and career ready.

Calderón, Trejo, and Montenegro (2016) state:

> Developments in neuroscience and learning theory point to the fact that a greater emphasis on building a caring community of learners, coupled with high expectations and challenging and engaging opportunities in the classroom, results in students becoming more reflective of their own emotions and relationships. These conditions enhance students' motivation to learn, which is directly linked to academic success (Schaps, Battistich, & Solomon, 2004).
>
> Joseph Durlak, Roger Weissberg, Allison Dymnicki, Rebecca Taylor, and Kriston Schellinger (2011) find that school-based universal interventions and their effect in enhancing students' social and emotional learning (SEL) supports the premise that cognitive, affective, and behavior skills are the foundation of academic success. In effect, students are more likely to express their creativity, curiosity, and empathy in environments where they feel included and safe. Students with developed SEL competencies will be better prepared for success in the 21st century. (pp. 12–13)

Note that ELs cannot participate fully in social and emotional learning activities that require English oral language discourse to express feelings and emotions unless they are explicitly taught in the same manner as you would teach academic vocabulary. ELs benefit greatly when they are able to collaborate with peers to learn academic language (Committee on the Study of Teacher Preparation Programs in the United States, 2010). For example, cooperative learning strategies, whether students are in pairs, triads, or quads, are most effective when norms of collaboration are clearly defined in the context of developing social and emotional learning competencies such as building relationships, valuing diversity, and showing empathy for students who are not proficient in English. With their peers, ELs need to be given ample opportunities to practice higher-order discourse, paired reading, and team writing exercises so they can see other models of vocabulary and language use.

Teachers and administrators can best teach and embed social and emotional skills into the instructional framework by becoming knowledgeable of the five core social and emotional learning competencies.

Five Core Social and Emotional Learning Competencies

CASEL (2013) identifies five core social and emotional learning competencies that can help EL students strengthen their cognitive, affective, and behavioral skills. (See figure 3.1, page 55.)

1. **Self-awareness:** The ability to accurately recognize one's feelings and thoughts and their influence on behaviors, which includes assessing one's strengths and limitations and possessing a well-grounded sense of self-efficacy and optimism. This includes being aware of one's own bias and prejudices toward other cultures, language groups, and races.

2. **Self-management:** The ability to regulate one's emotions, thoughts, and behaviors effectively in different situations, which includes delaying gratification, managing stress, controlling impulses, motivating oneself, and setting and working toward personal and academic goals. This includes refraining from making rash judgments or negative comments about children from other cultures, or those who come from poverty.

3. **Social awareness:** The ability to take the perspective of and empathize with others from diverse backgrounds and cultures, to understand social and ethical norms for behavior, and to recognize family, school, and community resources and supports. This includes being culturally

responsive in developing lessons that are inclusive and represent the diverse populations in a classroom and school.

4. **Relationship skills:** The ability to establish and maintain healthy and rewarding relationships with diverse individuals and groups, which includes communicating clearly, listening actively, cooperating, resisting inappropriate social pressure, negotiating conflict constructively, and seeking help when needed. This includes facilitating healthy interactions among students from diverse backgrounds and encouraging them to be more inclusive outside of the classroom, on the playground, in the cafeteria, or in clubs.

5. **Responsible decision making:** The ability to make constructive choices about personal behavior, social interactions, and school, which includes considering ethical standards, safety concerns, social norms, the consequences of various actions, and the well-being of self and others.

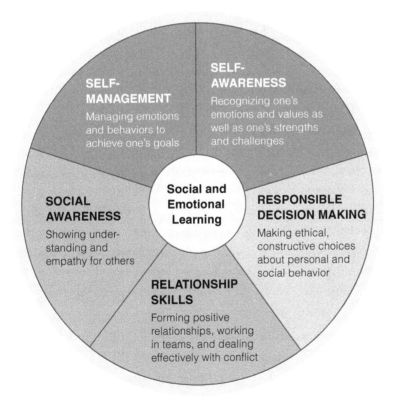

Source: CASEL, 2013. Used with permission.

Figure 3.1: Five core social and emotional learning competencies.

Explicitly teaching social and emotional skills is essential to meeting state academic standards (Adams, 2013). Emphasizing that students develop a broad range of skills that include cognitive, social, and emotional competencies helps them to be successful in work and life. For example, Common Core State Standards ask students to be proficient in many social and emotional skills, including (NGA & CCSSO, 2010a, 2010b):

- Reflecting on the meaning of their own learning
- Managing their personal resources to achieve goals
- Working collaboratively and cooperatively with others on collective tasks
- Participating in relationship-centered learning activities that involve engagement and language skills
- Using problem-solving and decision-making skills to complete higher-order tasks

Through the use of interactive and cooperative learning activities, teachers can help students learn how to regulate their emotions, problem solve, disagree respectfully, collaborate with their peers, and see others' perspectives. For ELs, one of the most important social and emotional learning competencies to address in schools and in the classroom is empathy (CASEL, 2013). Smith, Fisher, and Frey (2015) state that, "Empathy is the ability to accurately identify the emotional states of others and respond to them with care and concern" (p. 43). A school community that takes the *perspective of and empathizes with others from diverse backgrounds and cultures* is one that establishes systems that welcome newcomers and their families into the school, provides services in a friendly and culturally sensitive manner to ensure that students receive appropriate placements, and trains teachers to be prepared to meet the students' needs. This school strives to become knowledgeable of school and community resources and supports that facilitate the newcomers' transition into a new environment.

Crowley and Saide (2016), in their article "Building Empathy in Classrooms and Schools," make a compelling argument that empathizing with others from diverse backgrounds is a complex concept and a difficult skill. Empathy is a *soft skill* that, in this era of high-stakes testing and accountability, is not always valued, much less explicitly taught. To feel empathy toward others from different cultures and backgrounds requires one to take a critical look at one's own biases and prejudices to better understand one's feelings toward others. Empathy involves celebrating, on a regular basis, the unique qualities and talents that each student brings to school and acknowledging, validating, and embedding these unique qualities into the daily routines and practices of the classroom.

Modeling and facilitating empathy in the classroom may be difficult, but doing so is essential to creating a climate and culture that validates everyone and excludes no one (Crowley & Saide, 2016). Unfortunately, lack of empathy, knowledge, and sensitivity to the different circumstances of ELs results in students being locked into a system of low expectations, unqualified staff, and misaligned resources that dampens their motivation to succeed. Furthermore, there exist institutional mindsets that are inflexible and unable to adapt to the academic and emotional needs, learning styles, and cultural differences that ELs bring to schools. For the most part, the faculty and staff do not share the language, culture, and values of the EL population, therefore making it difficult for them to fully understand the critical need for them to adjust their curriculum and pedagogy, and create a climate and culture in their classrooms to be more inclusive and nurturing. With the rapid influx of ELs and diverse populations into schools throughout the country, social and emotional competencies should not be viewed as random acts of empathy or even considered optional, but embedded in all levels of the school, from the front office to the cafeteria to the classrooms.

Levels of Schoolwide Social and Emotional Learning

The most effective approach to make social and emotional learning systemic is for the leadership team to place value on and model SEL competencies schoolwide. Taking it a step further, fully integrating social and emotional learning in the academic program and across all systems, in preschool through high school, also provides opportunities for (CASEL, 2013):

- Establishing a powerful, relationship-centered approach to education
- Putting the social and emotional development of young people at the heart of every classroom and school

- Linking and integrating academic, social, and emotional learning in meaningful ways that support the full spectrum of students' development
- Enhancing student learning by increasing students':
  - Motivation to achieve
  - Ability to be attentive and engaged in the learning process
  - Satisfaction with learning
  - Sense of belonging
- Fostering the development of essential life skills

CASEL (2013) identifies three levels of social and emotional learning implementation: (1) classroom, (2) school, and (3) family and community. Each level focuses on different explicit skills and competencies that encourage all members of the school to participate and feel valued. Beginning at the classroom level, social and emotional skills and competencies should be embedded in course content and instructional strategies so that all students are engaged in the learning process. Students should be afforded the opportunity to practice social and emotional skills with their peers while learning the content and practicing academic language in a safe and supportive learning environment. A hands-on science lesson, an engaging math problem, or a team approach to a class project can be a rich, highly motivating language learning opportunity. Building on EL experiences and guiding them to reading and writing about history, literature, math, and science engages them in purposeful, guided instructional conversations about their learning experiences. Teachers reinforce social and emotional skills by valuing the students' cultural and language background by modeling inclusive behaviors that encourage other students to also value the diversity within their classroom.

Adults model social and emotional learning competencies throughout the building by cultivating positive and cooperative relationships with each other, with students, and with parents, even if they don't speak English. School policies and practices reflect the norms, beliefs, and practices that are established through an inclusive and collaborative process that involves all members of the school community, including the families of ELs. Changes in practices include: faculty and staff participating collectively in welcoming all students, family members, and community representatives into the school; actively encouraging the participation of family and community in school-related events, in a language that they understand; and increasing parent engagement and awareness of school operations, expectations, and how best to support their children in the learning process through a series of parent newsletters, parent training academies, and home visits.

Implementing social and emotional learning core competencies is just the beginning of helping EL students and their classmates develop strong social-emotional learning skills while excelling academically in all subject areas. Practices such as cooperative learning activities, cultivation of helping behaviors among peers, and adopting instructional practices that promote cultural responsiveness all promote and accelerate academic learning in the classroom.

Cooperative Learning Activities

Cooperative learning activities are an effective way to promote social and emotional learning at the classroom level as well as enhance academic performance. ELs at all levels of language proficiency benefit from the opportunity to learn and practice social and emotional competences through this approach because they can work in small-group settings, have multiple opportunities to use either language, make mistakes and take risks in smaller settings, and learn from peers who are at various academic and language levels.

All students, especially ELs, grow together academically and socially when teachers use cooperative learning strategies to achieve 100 percent student participation and practice time; exchange ideas; promote discourse and engagement in academic dialogue to express, summarize, and synthesize information; and develop team and individual accountability. The context in which students learn is just as important as the content they learn. Incorporating cooperative learning strategies in the content areas allows teachers to check the ELs' understanding, determine what they need to reteach, and assess the degree of their participation (Calderón et al., 1998). This book includes numerous instructional strategies that are highly engaging and interactive and that enrich the learning environment for ELs.

The most successful schools incorporate cooperative learning strategies as a part of a systemic approach to enhance English language acquisition, motivate students to want to learn in a safe and supportive learning community, and promote students' social and emotional development. These schools (Calderón, 2011b):

- Expedite language acquisition and academic progress
- Create student-centered learning environments, opportunities for differentiated instruction, integrated lesson development and experiences, and interactive grouping practices
- Promote inclusiveness and acceptance of all students
- Provide maximum opportunities for ELs to practice social and academic language in safe and supportive environments

Cooperative learning strategies that support ELs and integrate social and emotional learning are most effective when they meet each of the following standards (Calderón, 2011b).

- Teachers establish learning norms and protocols so students know what teachers expect of them during each activity.
- Teachers give students tasks, not roles, for performance during each lesson.
- Strategies for cooperative learning and classroom management go hand in hand, helping students to become more academically productive, better behaved, and less likely to drop out.

Adopting learning activities that foster cooperation between students works best when educators also ensure that students understand how to help each other.

Cultivation of Helping Behaviors

A social and emotional learning classroom with ELs is one in which teachers develop and maintain a safe, supportive, and well-managed learning environment where students feel cared for, respected, and challenged. This is the type of classroom climate in which ELs flourish (Calderón et al., 2016). ELs need to feel secure enough to raise their hands, take risks, and participate in class like everyone else.

A school climate that is safe for students to ask for help does not happen by accident. It has to be cultivated intentionally. Mara Sapon-Shevin (2010) identifies the helping curriculum that addresses four basic questions.

1. Did you ask for help today when you needed it?

2. Did you offer help to another when you recognized that he or she needed it?

3. Did you accept help when it was offered to you?

4. If you declined help, did you do it politely?

These helping behaviors are essential components of a cooperative, inclusive classroom and school, and they are at the heart of a social and emotional learning environment. If taught explicitly and practiced regularly, helping behaviors could be the catalyst that establishes and sustains a caring, safe classroom culture. These behaviors are essential for cooperative learning and group work to be successful. Helping strategies would also give English-dominant students the permission, license, and inspiration to assist others.

Of course, helping behaviors are just one aspect of student interaction that fosters strong social and emotional growth in the classroom. Your educators must also adopt instructional processes that reinforce the value to students of having different cultural backgrounds in the classroom.

Instructional Practices That Promote Cultural Responsiveness

Important to promoting systemic schoolwide social and emotional learning is using culturally responsive instructional practices that reflect the language and culture of ELs. *Culturally responsive teaching* is using the cultural characteristics, experiences, and perspectives of ethnically diverse students as a means for teaching them more effectively. Researchers describe three themes as a framework to enhance teachers' cultural responsiveness (CASEL, 2013).

1. **Multicultural awareness** requires a teacher to examine his or her own biases and assumptions about the culture, language, and behavior of students.

2. **Multicultural knowledge** is developed when teachers actively try to learn about each student's cultural background, including values that help shape the ways they deal with feelings, conflict, social interactions, social norms, and individual learning styles. Talk with them; have them share experiences; do your own research. One especially important and effective way to get to know about the family and culture is to conduct home visits.

3. **Multicultural skills** are appropriate strategies for working with students from diverse cultural backgrounds. Teachers who employ such skills create classroom communities where diverse students respect and support one another (see figure 3.2). Students discuss and value their differences and view cultural conflicts as opportunities for learning. All students benefit from interacting with students from other cultures. In this way, English speakers become more tolerant and learn to value diversity.

Figure 3.2: Student work from a classroom that emphasizes the value of diverse student backgrounds.

Conclusion

The integration of social and emotional learning competencies into the climate and culture of a school benefits all students and adults regardless of socioeconomic background, culture, and country of origin or language. The ability to be sensitive to the presence and respond to the needs of ELs must be intentional and supported by a framework that guides the thinking and practices of educators at all levels. The five core social and emotional learning competencies is that framework. It provides the foundation that accelerates learning and increases future possibilities for all ELs. When integrated systemically into the core content, social and emotional learning can motivate students to want to learn and help them feel included, experience less stress, and demonstrate fewer behavioral problems that disrupt the learning environment. Coupled with ExC-ELL strategies that focus on academic language designed to increase reading and writing skills of ELs, social and emotional learning enables teachers to enrich the learning environment, making it safe for all students to learn, feel included, and feel that their language and culture are respected and valued.

Discussion Questions

Consider the following.

- Have you offered professional development on social and emotional learning to your staff at the school or district level?
- Have you offered professional development on cooperative learning and social and emotional learning to your teachers?
- How can you involve your language minority parents in multicultural awareness, which helps their child academically, as well as in social and emotional skill development events and training?

CHAPTER 4

Professional Development Components

Training

Academic definition: A process by which people learn the skills they need for an art, profession, or job

Friendly definition: To make ready for a skill

The purpose of professional development is to improve student achievement. The best way to improve instructional practices in schools is through professional development that includes evidence-based knowledge (Darling-Hammond, 2009; Guskey, 2010; Hargreaves & Fullan, 2012) with follow-up coaching (Calderón, 1984; Joyce & Showers, 1996, 2002), and participation in a professional learning community (PLC) (DuFour, 2004) or teacher learning community (TLC) (Calderón, 1990–1991, 1999). The schools we work with begin to integrate ELs into their PLCs as well as TLCs, creating a culture of collaboration to ensure that ELs are part of the school improvement efforts. Throughout this book, we focus more on teams working in TLCs, which have the ability to focus exclusively and specifically on the instructional needs of ELs and the students in the classrooms with ELs. General education teachers and ESL teachers work together in TLCs. In essence, effective implementation of any instructional program requires a comprehensive professional development effort with all educators in the school totally committed. This is especially true for programs with a diversity of ELs that must demonstrate success. This chapter examines *why* ELs have not been successful in schools and presents *how* schools are now creating success for ELs and all students, teachers, and administrators.

What Research Says About Most English Learner Instruction

Many possible factors contribute to the poor performance of ELs, but researchers point to the under-preparedness of mainstream teachers to meet the demands of the rapidly growing EL population (Gándara, 2005; Gonzalez, Yawkey, & Minaya-Rowe, 2006; Walqui & van Leir, 2010). Dorothy S. Strickland and Donna E. Alvermann (2004) suggest that much of the low achievement of language minority students may be pedagogically induced or exacerbated.

Robert E. Slavin and colleagues (2009) remind us that the key contributing factor to the achievement gap is a discrepancy in the quality of instruction students receive. At the elementary level, many well-implemented bilingual and ESL programs facilitate the progress of minority students, but others provide low levels of challenge and shield students from the curriculum necessary for successful placement at the next level of schooling (Valdes, 1997). Valdes emphasizes that a business-as-usual approach to literacy instruction results in failure for EL students.

Through our work with schools, we find that the quality of instruction for ELs is complicated by the following factors.

- Many EL teachers feel unprepared to teach basic reading, reading comprehension skills, or subjects that schools sometimes offer as sheltered courses (sheltered math, sheltered science, or sheltered social studies) where the content is simplified in order for some students to understand. Often, the ESL teachers do not have core content certification.

- Many elementary schools send students into middle school without having exited LEP status. In other words, these schools produce long-term ELs. Middle and high school content teachers need to be specially prepared to address the needs of these EL students.

- Many reading teachers are not prepared to teach reading to adolescent ELs. Some ELs are coming to secondary schools with preliteracy or low-literacy skills, even in their native languages. Students with interrupted formal education (SIFE) need special interventions before they can participate in the reading interventions the school or district offers or make sense of their mainstream content courses.

- The culture of some schools has created a chasm between ESL specialists and mainstream content teachers. This lack of interaction and collaboration prevents collegial learning and instructional improvement for all teachers and ELs.

Perhaps a great teacher of ELs in your school has already surpassed hurdles because he or she was the only teacher at that school who taught ELs. The teacher probably had to figure things out alone while having to convince reluctant colleagues they also had the responsibility. The one EL teacher or handful of EL teachers became smart and talented by committing to students and colleagues. Their moral purpose became the relentless pursuit of learning and a desire to always do better for ELs. They tried for years not to be disheartened in spite of having little help and little recognition. In scenarios like this one, it is vital to bring these teachers to the forefront and enlist their talents and love of ELs to assist in the whole-school transition to meet ELs' needs; doing so will have a positive impact on many other students.

Bruce Joyce and Beverly Showers (1996) gathered two hundred studies on professional development. Based on this review, they developed a report on training processes and outcomes that are still forming the foundation of current effective professional development practices. They find the following major training elements in the most successful programs.

- Presentation of theory, research, and description of skills or strategy
- Demonstration of skills or the model of teaching
- Practice in simulated classroom settings
- Feedback—structured or open ended
- Coaching for application

Once teachers learn a teaching skill, they need to adapt it to the conditions of the classroom in order to have significant impact on the academic achievement of students (August et al., 2008; Joyce & Showers, 1996). In earlier studies, Calderón (1984) and Marsh and Calderón (1989) find that ESL, bilingual, and sheltered English instruction teachers need follow-up systems that enable them to accomplish each of the following.

- Reflect more systematically on the effects of their teaching on their students
- Have time to try new combinations of teaching skills and strategies with colleagues
- Adjust to the different levels of students, situations, and subject matter
- Learn how to work collaboratively through peer coaching and contribute to teachers' learning communities or professional learning communities in their schools

Before planning professional development, you might want to review or update data on the teachers' credentials. Use figure 4.1 (page XX) to tally how many teachers you have in each area.

Teachers With One or More ELs	Number
EL teachers with ESL or ELD credentials or certification	
Core content or mainstream teachers with ESL or ELD credentials or certification	
Special education teachers	
Literacy or mathematics coaches with ESL or ELD credentials or certification	
Teachers with specialized training to teach ELs	
Administrators with ESL or ELD credentials or certification	

Figure 4.1: Tally of teachers who work with ELs.

*Visit **go.SolutionTree.com/EL** for a free reproducible version of this figure.*

A Comprehensive Professional Development Model

For teachers to achieve the type of complex learning described in chapters 2 and 3, they need support, opportunities for collaboration at professional development workshops and at school, and tools to help them reflect on how their own progress affects their students' development. Schools should plan comprehensive professional development for EL achievement in a two-year loop as seen in figure 4.2. This loop facilitates teacher accumulation of learned knowledge from declarative to procedural to conditional.

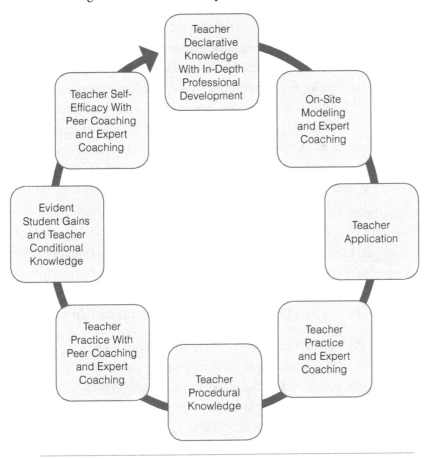

Figure 4.2: Two-year professional development model.

Types of Learned Knowledge

Declarative knowledge is the ability for teachers to talk about what they learned in the training; *procedural knowledge* is the ability to deliver the instructional sequence with fidelity; and *conditional knowledge* is knowing how to gauge what works with particular students and being able to adjust instruction to meet those needs.

Some teachers have the disposition and skill to move faster through the two-year loop from declarative knowledge to procedural knowledge and finally to conditional knowledge, where they adapt their teaching to the students' learning needs. They only need a year of PD. Many teachers, however, require the full two years to effectively make these transitions. Experience is not generally a factor in this process because both experienced and novice teachers come with a range of knowledge, skills, and dispositions. Therefore, expert coaches must work with teachers as individuals. Some teachers need to see the experts teach their class; others want constant technical feedback on both their and their students' performance.

Although this two-year loop is the norm, teachers that can, in just one year, develop the knowledge and skill to apply the new strategies, learn to adjust the procedures to their teaching styles, and adapt those skills to whatever condition is necessary to their individual ELs' needs or to the current curricula frameworks, will have a greater impact on ELs by being able to accomplish the following.

- Plan and design lessons (where and how to teach vocabulary, reading skills, peer-practice activities, and so on) within the school's or district's current literacy programs, mathematics programs, STEM frameworks, or other curricula.

- Deliver instruction, integrating language and literacy within each content area.

- Reflect on the delivery and design of lessons (determine what was actually delivered and the quality of each instructional event).

- Record authentic student performance to analyze how and where teaching affects ELs' successes—and where it's lacking.

Teachers on this cycle set out to accomplish the following four goals: (1) engage in professional development and coaching, (2) develop knowledge about teaching ELs, (3) implement quality instruction, and (4) ensure student achievement (see figure 4.3).

| Professional Development Training and Sustained Coaching | Teacher Knowledge | Quality Instruction | Student Achievement |

Figure 4.3: Goals for teachers to accomplish.

Again, many teachers can fulfill these goals within a single year, while others require a second year to accomplish them, repeating this cycle to get better academic results. Therefore, it is important to repeat some workshops or offer abbreviated versions. For some teachers, preteaching vocabulary in only ten minutes is a challenge. Some mathematics, science, and social studies teachers have difficulty letting go and letting their students practice the words and discourse with a peer. Most secondary teachers need a review of the reading process and how to consolidate language, literacy, and content. Schools can conduct frequent follow-up refresher workshops in one- or two-hour sessions to serve as reminders—or as instigators of new insights.

Ensuring Transfer From Training to Classrooms

Ensuring transfer from a solid, well-designed training program, like the one we described in chapter 2, requires extensive follow-up through a combination of options, including the following.

- Differentiated coaching by expert coaches
- Co-teaching by ESL and general education teacher
- TLC focused on ELs
- Peer coaching across disciplines
- Use of ExC-ELL or a similar observation protocol by all for lesson planning and self-reflection

- Training of school-based teacher leaders as coaches and trainers of other teachers
- Teacher support by school leadership

Although this chapter focuses on coaching, co-teaching, and establishing a meaningful TLC, chapters 5 and 6 detail the use of observational tools for coaching and evaluating teachers and the role of the school's leadership.

Here we look more closely at how the predictability of transfer from training, observation tools, and teacher support systems affect transition to classrooms.

We can predict the impact on teachers and subsequently on students based on the professional development program design and the amount of expert coaching that each teacher receives. One useful metric is to identify competency gained by separating learned knowledge into categories as seen in chapter 2 and in the Types of Learned Knowledge feature box in this chapter.

Using an Observational Tool

Classroom observations require systematic observation tools. Expert coaches, peer coaches, and administrators need to be on the same page when it comes to observations. The observation protocols and tools need to be specific enough to capture what the teachers learned from professional development. A way to test the validity and reliability of an observation tool for classrooms with ELs is to ask questions such as the following.

- "Do all observers walk out of a classroom having reached consensus on what they observed?"
- "Do observers reach consensus when they use the protocol?"
- "Is the protocol or tool reliable across the content areas and diverse ESL and ELD classrooms?"

The ExC-ELL observation protocol and its abbreviated form for walkthroughs—the WISEcard—have been tested for validity and reliability in New York City and Kauai during the five-year Carnegie study. The following groups use protocols such as the WISEcard in various ways.

- Teachers:
    - As a template for planning content lessons that integrate language, literacy, and content
    - To record EL performance and track EL progress
    - To reflect on the delivery of their instruction and how it correlates with the students observed during that class period
    - When observing and coaching each other to facilitate change, reaffirm effective practices, and sustain motivation
- Literacy coaches when they need to coach teachers with ELs
- Supervisors and administrators to identify quality instruction and reward teachers
- Researchers for conducting classroom research on fidelity of implementation, patterns of effective or ineffective instruction, and teacher-student learning connections

Creating Teacher Support Systems

To set a context for the transfer from training, we propose the following teacher support mechanisms.

- A requirement that all site coaches and administrators attend the three-day professional development on teaching vocabulary, reading, and writing with core content or an abbreviated version on the instructional model and how to support teachers through their experimental phase
- A requirement that all site coaches and administrators attend a session on how to use the observation protocol and how to shadow the trainers during observations in order to help coaches and administrators feel comfortable with the observation protocol
- Systematic observations to identify potential trainers and coaches from the schools, who would continue to sustain the innovation after the project

A teacher-oriented program also provides low-risk practice sessions in a workshop setting where teachers can practice teaching strategies in small teams, modeling the way school-based teams work in a TLC. An evidence-based professional development program that is comprehensive in its content and process also includes training educators on how to work in a TLC to apply the new learning and how to use an observational protocol to measure transfer from training and impact on students (Calderón, 1999).

Coaching helps change the culture of teaching and learning. It creates fidelity with ownership and fidelity to an innovation with regard to the whole-school goal of implementing a specific set of strategies. It helps sustain quality implementation. When done right, coaching helps everyone become a learner—the observed and the observer. It is a vehicle for updating the curriculum. Most important, it improves student achievement by opening classrooms for everyone to see and learn from.

Funds Required to Plan for Comprehensive Professional Development

In order for teachers and coaches to meet expectations, schools must consider professional development designs and allocate funds for coaching from the initial training all the way through to the classroom. Funding coaching in the classroom is particularly important given that schools are often accustomed to spending large amounts on a few workshops but not necessarily on the follow-up embedded learning. Ongoing learning may cost as much as or more than the initial professional development; however, this is what yields results. You can use a worksheet like the one in figure 4.4 (page 75) to help you calculate the costs of professional development targeted at supporting ELs.

Training Topic	Days of Professional Development	Costs	Number of Participants	Number of Coaching Days (Six Teachers per Day)	Cost for Coaching
Vocabulary					
Reading					
Writing					
Cooperative learning and social and emotional learning					
Lesson development					
Session for coaches					
Session for administrators					
Refresher workshops					
TLC focused on ELs					
Co-teaching					

Figure 4.4: Budget projections.

*Visit **go.SolutionTree.com/EL** for a free reproducible version of this figure.*

Once the school determines goals for the different teacher cohorts, it can chart the desired skills and observable outcomes, as in figure 4.5 (page 76).

Status **C:** Completed **IP:** In progress **OH:** On hold	Desired Outcomes	Next Steps
	1. Teachers plan and implement appropriate reading strategies through guided reading and centering activities for ELs at different levels of English language proficiency.	
	2. Teachers in preK to fifth grade explicitly teach phonemic and phonological awareness, decoding, vocabulary, and reading comprehension specific to ELs' development.	
	3. Teachers in sixth to twelfth grades identify reading comprehension, language, and content objectives and explicitly model how to apply during reading.	
	4. Teachers of students with interrupted formal education and newcomers (levels 1 and 2) use targeted reading strategies relevant to the individual needs of these students.	
	5. All teachers in the school incorporate strategies for vocabulary development, reading comprehension skills, and writing skills in their lessons and instructional delivery.	
	6. K–12 sheltered English instruction, ESL, and students with interrupted formal education teachers use a variety of performance assessments and ways of measuring learning progressions on content learning, academic vocabulary, reading, and writing development.	
	7. All teachers plan and deliver writing instruction and activities relevant to their subject matter.	
	8. Teachers develop different rubrics for writing that are appropriate for ELs at different proficiency levels and that keep track of learning progressions.	

Figure 4.5: Skills and observable outcomes.

*Visit **go.SolutionTree.com/EL** for a free reproducible version of this figure.*

Using the Status column should be fairly straightforward. You should determine the content for the Next Steps column based on the results of the professional development relative to the goals for each step. Those outcomes will determine how you can best follow up this training.

Immediate and Intentional Follow-Up to Training

As soon as possible after training, you need to return to your team or TLC and establish your path forward. Highlight the tasks your team needs to accomplish. These tasks generally involve the following.

- Examining student performance data in the various content areas such as literature, social studies, mathematics, and science
- Analyzing student progress against the content and performance standards in a timely manner
- Identifying student strengths and needs
- Discussing implementation of the new model, including how often and how teachers use it
- Aligning the curriculum with district standards and grade-level materials
- Sharing or reviewing teaching strategies
- Sharing areas of success—and areas for improvement
- Having open conversations regarding beliefs and biases about EL students

Teachers need to generate and plan TLC activities, adaptable to their emergent needs (providing collective autonomy), and scheduled as part of the work day, work week, and school's calendar. Ensuring that these activities maintain a high level of quality requires the following.

- Establishing quality interaction norms with common ground rules to allow everyone to participate
- Scheduling continual training that includes teamwork, trust building, and team building to re-energize and refocus the groups to ensure success

- Keeping TLC activities brief:
  - Five minutes for sharing successes
  - Five minutes for problem solving
  - Ten or fifteen minutes for instructional demos or for analyzing student work
  - Five minutes for celebration
- Self-assessing performance within TLCs; reporting their accomplishments to the principal on a monthly basis
- Requiring systematic administrator participation that includes praising teachers and identifying areas of difficulty or need
- Celebrating periodically to recognize the TLCs' successes

Successful TLCs concentrate on meeting teachers' individual needs. Even when a teacher prefers to work alone on action research or online learning and inquiry projects, he or she still needs support, specific plans, and timelines. Such teachers can work alone but should still periodically share in TLCs.

Here are further examples of activities that teachers may find best suit them.

- Peer coaching, wherein teachers observe each other teach and give feedback
- Working in small groups on curriculum, lesson development, exchange of lessons, professional book studies, video analysis, and alignment
- Analyzing student data, figuring out gaps, and laying out plans for instructional interventions, including monitoring teacher and student progress

Activities like these are all a means to stimulate conversation among colleagues in their TLCs or PLCs. These team conversations should prioritize these elements of ELs' learning progressions in vocabulary usage, reading comprehension, and writing on a monthly basis. Use these topics to discuss and monitor:

- Linguistic development
- Reading development

- Writing development
- Core concept development
- Significant gaps in development
- Cultural challenges
- Social and emotional challenges
- Analysis of student factors and artifacts in order to change practice

In the past, only ESL teachers discussed these topics, and even then only if there were two or more ESL teachers at the campus. For the most part, only one teacher serviced fifty to sixty students or more. Sometimes, the ESL teacher might have informal conversations with the core content teacher(s). However, since EL populations have grown exponentially and federal laws are asking for everyone to get involved, from faculty and administration to student family members, educators are now moving to whole-school participation and ownership of these discussions. In addition to meeting in TLCs and PLCs, partnerships between ESL and content teachers are forming. Team teaching and co-teaching is one of the most promising practices.

Professional Development for Co-Teaching

Ideally, all ESL and general education teachers should team teach. That is, both take turns being the lead teacher for the whole class. However, in some cases, ESL and general education teachers work together in the classroom but not in the most productive manner. In these cases, the role of the ESL teacher may seem unclear and unproductive. In one school, the ESL teacher told us that he "mills around and helps other students because the ELs don't like to be singled out. The principal had to talk to the class about that not being a stigma" (M. Roberts, personal communication, March 24, 2015). Whereas in another school, it was difficult to distinguish between the three teachers: who was the ESL, the special education teacher, and the general education teacher? They all took active roles in teaching and facilitating. The professional development strand on co-teaching for ESL and core content teachers can include these elements.

- Joint planning (which means giving school time for it)

- Curriculum mapping and alignment
- Parallel teaching (for example, addressing the same theme, genre, essential questions, standards, and key vocabulary; fostering reading skills; building background; and reviewing key concepts)
- Co-developing complementary materials
- Assessing student work collaboratively
- Using one or more of the co-teaching or collaborative models of teaching:
  - Both teachers direct the class. The core teacher teaches; the ESL teacher provides examples, clarifies, uses visuals, restates, and so on.
  - Teachers switch roles so that each gets half of the class time. The core teacher teaches, and the ESL teacher monitors or assesses students. Then, they switch roles.
  - The class is divided in half and both teach the same content to a heterogeneous group. Both teachers are well skilled in sheltering content.
  - The ESL teacher preteaches vocabulary; the core teacher presents the concepts, and the ESL teacher asks or clarifies questions, elicits summaries from students, and reinforces use of new vocabulary.
  - Both teachers teach multiple groups by switching groups every twenty minutes or so.
  - Both teachers manage classroom routines (taking attendance, distributing materials, giving instructions, keeping discipline, and so on).

Once the professional development and the follow-up support mechanisms are in place, the biggest challenge is to sustain the quality of their implementation. Other challenges will emerge, including how to gauge what is working well and what needs to be modified. Student data will show the level of progress for students, while classroom observation protocols will show the level of progress for teachers. In chapter 6 (page 99) we discuss how to communicate whole-school expectations for knowledge transfer from the training received in the professional development sessions to classroom instruction.

How to Monitor and Measure Implementation for Positive Transfer From the Training Into the Classroom

Monitoring and measuring teacher implementation means documenting educator learning and its impact on students. The school should track each teacher's learning progression throughout the year. Without documenting the level of transfer from the training into the teacher's instructional repertoire or the implementation of the training in each classroom, we cannot determine why students (particularly ELs) are not learning.

A monitoring instrument needs specificity on how teachers conduct academic language, reading comprehension, and writing instruction within the subject areas as well as on the quality of the students' application of that instruction verbally, for reading comprehension, and in their writing. Special tools that contains all the attributes of ExC-ELL are necessary to store data, analyze data, and find relationships between instruction and student performance in order to make instructional and systems recommendations.

For appropriate training, school administrators and peer coaches or specialist coaches shadow the expert coaches during class observations. Administrators and other school leaders attend the coaching professional development with their teachers, plus one additional day of training on building teacher support systems, using observation protocols, and giving feedback to teachers. After attending the professional development on coaching, the administrators and coaches shadow the expert consultants or coaches to reinforce their learning about coaching.

How Administrators Support Coaches and Teachers

School administrators also participate in their own sessions focused on systematically monitoring and measuring implementation. After training, administrators should shadow the ExC-ELL experts two or three times to compare class observations. The observation protocols and ancillary tools they use for this purpose should generate data that they can use to graph and track learning by the teachers and students throughout the year. School administrators also need to schedule the support systems. Then they, along with the faculty, can analyze quarterly reports to make adjustments. End-of-year reports should consist of individual teacher growth data, student outcomes, and school factors that facilitated or impeded growth.

As we visit schools during implementation, we constantly hear from principals who shadow us, "I learned so much about instruction today!" "These visits brought me back to the reason I became a principal." "Now I see how it all goes together." "Wow, why weren't we having all of our teachers do this before?"

The next chapters elaborate on the administrators' role during the implementation phase. Their messages, knowledge about ELs, and support mechanisms will be central to a quality implementation.

Conclusion

The professional development does not end after a workshop or a comprehensive institute where teachers, coaches, and administrators are trained on evidence-based EL instruction. Moreover, the additional training of coaches and administrators on how to support teachers will sustain the innovation when well implemented. Implementation is the critical phase. Coaching each teacher should begin within the first six weeks after the training by expert coaches, site coaches, and administrators. Chapter 5 goes into detail about the coaching process and tools.

Discussion Questions

Consider the following.

- Does your professional development on EL instruction consist of mainly one-shot workshops?
- Does your professional development consist of theory and demonstrations, teacher practice and feedback or reflection at the workshops, and lesson integration?
- What do you need to do to design and implement a two-year plan?
- How do you plan to make your professional development on EL instruction comprehensive, with at least four days of vocabulary, reading, writing, and lesson development?
- Do more lesson development, coaching, and TLC activities follow training to ensure transfer?

- What percentage of your professional development funds goes to workshops on different topics? To successive comprehensive workshops on EL instruction as described in chapter 2? To motivational speakers? To travel to conferences?
- How will you monitor implementation?
- Which co-teaching configuration will the ESL and general education teachers implement?

CHAPTER 5

Professional Coaching in the Classroom

Support mechanisms

Academic definition: A formal system or method of providing assistance

Friendly definition: An orderly plan for the process of achieving a goal

---

The training of school-based teacher leaders as coaches drives the effectiveness of their coaching, as does training that helps teachers understand the basis, motivation, and teacher-student benefits of coaching. Coaches need to interact with teachers to facilitate learning in their actual classrooms with their actual students on an ongoing basis. When coaches and teachers work as a team and are committed to creating success for both ELs and all other students, students and schools see tremendous growth (Joyce & Showers, 1996; Calderón, 1984). Unfortunately, effective implementation of coaching is somewhat formidable and challenging to sustain.

This chapter focuses on what research says about the effectiveness of professional coaching, what effective professional development for coaches looks like, and how to generate positive outcomes for coaches, teachers, and ELs in the classroom.

What Research Says About the Benefits of Peer Coaching

Joyce and Showers (1996, 2002) find that elementary and secondary teachers in peer-coaching relationships practice new skills more frequently, apply them more appropriately in their classrooms, demonstrate clearer understanding of the purposes and uses of new skills, and show greater retention and improvement in their use of new skills over time compared with teachers not in coaching relationships. Calderón (1984, 2007a) finds that when elementary and secondary core content teachers with ELs in their classrooms apply more academic vocabulary, reading comprehension, and writing strategies relevant to EL learning—all things peer-coaching relationships can facilitate—their ELs outperform ELs in compared control schools.

Another random-assignment study (Garet et al., 2008) tests the effectiveness of a professional development program complemented by coaching as one of two professional development interventions provided to second-grade teachers in high-poverty schools. The study finds that the professional development program with coaching does improve teachers' knowledge of scientifically based reading instruction and leads to greater use of one of the three desired instructional practices piloted in the study.

Professional Development for Coaches

We talked in depth in chapter 4 (page 65) about professional development strategies for teachers and administrators. Coaching comes with its own best practices and strategies that benefit from professional development time. In order for teachers to be open to coaching, coaches need to accomplish three things.

1. Develop a deep understanding of the reform they are helping to implement, particularly if it's a complex one such as ensuring academic success for ELs in all subject areas, as well as all other students.

2. Develop high levels of content skill as they go through the same training as the teachers.

3. Spend an additional day of training focused on how to conduct preconferences and observations, gather data

during observations, reflect on those data, present the data and technical feedback to the teacher, and jointly plan next steps with the teacher being coached.

The role of coaching also calls for interpersonal skills that:

- Facilitate companionship and personal relationships during this difficult process (for example, supportiveness, accessibility, respectfulness, flexibility, tactfulness, and trust and credibility)
- Analyze application and adaptation of the new instructional strategies to ELs and all other students in the classroom
- Tailor assistance to individual teachers' needs

Even well-prepared coaches face numerous challenges as they enter the school system. Their list of responsibilities and demands on time are many, which requires a great deal of planning and forethought to ensure students and teachers alike benefit from their knowledge.

Logistics for Scheduling the School Coach's Tasks

The not-so-easy job of coaching requires time and support to be successful. In some schools, the role of the EL or ELD coach expands into other tasks: assessing ELs and analyzing data; providing resources, materials, and lesson plans; setting up or facilitating workshops; and unfortunately, substituting for other teachers and helping with administrative tasks. Before long, the EL or ELD coach does not have time for coaching teachers. For this reason, it is critically important to write down specific tasks and to schedule the days each of those tasks is to be performed. The schedule—like the one in figure 5.1 (page 88)—must be posted for everyone, including administrators, to see and adhere to.

A coach can do a preconference, observation, and post conference with feedback and next steps with about five teachers in one day. Write the names of the teachers to be coached in the Monday, Wednesday, and Friday columns. Tuesday and Thursday columns are for the ESL coaches to schedule the other activities, meetings, or paperwork.

Monday	Tuesday	Wednesday	Thursday	Friday
Coach five teachers (preobservation, observation, and feedback session).	Assess EL students, analyze data, and meet with parents and school committees.	Coach five teachers (preobservation, observation, and feedback session).	Facilitate teamwork; guide resources and lesson development for teachers; coordinate site visits with expert coaches.	Coach two or more teachers, and if time allows, assist administration with other duties.
1. 2. 3. 4. 5.		1. 2. 3. 4. 5.		1. 2. 3. 4. 5.

Figure 5.1: Sample coaching schedule.

Visit **go.SolutionTree.com/EL** *for a free reproducible version of this figure.*

One important role of the school coach is to serve as the main contact between the school and the outside professional development consultants, trainers, and expert coaches. After the initial professional development session, expert coaches come to the school to conduct the first series of coaching. The expert coaches model the whole coaching process for site administrators and coaches. As the key contact, the school coach keeps in constant communication with the outside coaches to organize and facilitate the school visits, including ensuring that the administration and teachers under observation contribute to the schedules so that there are no surprises, that teachers have their lessons prepared, and that sufficient observation protocol forms are available for all who want to shadow the expert coaches.

Logistics for the Expert Coach's Visits

As part of the ExC-ELL coaching component, the following recommendations help school coaches organize the day of the visit.

- **Before the visit:** A week or three days before expert trainers and coaches visit, schools should do the following.

- Select six teacher volunteers to observe and coach.
- Submit the schedule for observations, coaching, debriefing, and planning with the teachers.
- Request that teachers email the lesson plan portion to all who will be participating in the observation, or to have a copy ready the morning of the observation.
- Invite a maximum of three teachers to one observation.
- Invite all site administrators to shadow the expert coach for all or some of the observations; encourage central administrators to attend.
- **During the visit, first meeting:** The day begins with a thirty-minute meeting with the principal, assistant principals, site coaches, coordinators, and the teachers to observe. The meeting should accomplish the following tasks.
  - Review the observation protocol.
  - Review and adjust the schedule for the day.
  - Prepare the leadership team to shadow the expert coaches and use the observation protocol during observations.
- **During the visit, observations:** Expert coaches can typically observe six teachers for ten- to fifteen-minute intervals in each classroom—five minutes for a preobservation, at least fifteen minutes for feedback with each teacher afterwards, and five minutes to get to the next classroom. An example schedule would then look like:
  - 9:00—Preobservation conference with teacher 1
  - 9:10—Observation
  - 9:25—Postobservation feedback
  - 9:45—Preobservation conference with teacher 2

Another option is to have two or more expert coaches visit the same day in order to visit more teachers. More options for expert coaches to help teachers include the following.

- **Refresher workshop:** If there is time at the end of the day, or another convenient time, conduct a *refresher workshop* for thirty to forty-five minutes to review some of the strategies presented at the training. The schedule should indicate this.

- **Co-teaching preparation:** If co-teaching a lesson with the expert coach is part of the plan, send copies of the lesson and the portion of the text the students will be reading to the expert coach in order to prepare for the co-teaching. Make sure students sit accordingly for the selected strategy if it is cooperative learning in teams or partner reading in pairs or triads, and that all supplies are ready and waiting.

- **Substitute teachers:** Schools typically hire a substitute to afford time for these brief observations and to cover the observed teachers' classes as they receive feedback from the expert coaches.

- **Use of technology:** If teachers and administration are comfortable with being videotaped, then do so. The video enhances the feedback session for the teachers because they get to see themselves and their students in action. The expert coach should leave the videos with the teachers. The school would need to secure parental permission if students are to be included.

- **Use of e-coaching:** If teachers video themselves, some expert coaches provide feedback online to uploaded clips or provide feedback during following visits.

Observations and coaching are not limited to classroom observations. Many highly effective coaching sessions occur outside the classroom. Here are a few typical observation formats plus a few suggestions in other settings.

- **Observation of a teacher implementing a strategy:** The expert coach observes and gives feedback on a specific strategy such as 7 Steps, think-aloud, partner reading and summarization, Numbered Heads Together, Roundtable, Write Around, Ratiocination, and Cut and Grow. The teacher selects the focus of the observation.

- **Observation of students applying a strategy:** As the teacher conducts a lesson, such as 7 Steps vocabulary, partner reading, or summarization, the expert coach observes and collects information on the students' application.

- **Strategy sharing:** During a thirty-minute TLC meeting, one or two teachers share a five-minute strategy that has worked for them, and three or four other teachers ask questions or add other success stories. The expert coach adds to the strategies.

- **Lesson designs:** An expert coach helps a teacher develop or refine a lesson, and site coaches and administrators participate.

- **Peer coaching:** If two teachers want to observe each other and give each other feedback, an expert coach can show them the protocol for peer coaching, giving constructive feedback, and setting goals.

- **Meetings in TLCs or PLCs:** Expert coaches meet with a team or conduct grade-level meetings to answer questions on effective strategies, modeling a strategy, or problem solving or to celebrate successes.

- **Authentic or performance assessment:** A teacher studies an aspect of his or her students' learning by recording their performance over a period of time. The expert coach guides this process.

Employing multiple observation formats helps gauge teacher progress, but that progress also hinges on ensuring that teachers buy into the coach-teacher dynamic.

Differentiated Coaching by Expert and School Coaches

Because teachers are the ultimate implementers, buy-in for coaching is critical. Some teachers exhibit resistance. Others may want to wait in hopes that the whole project fizzles out. That leaves only a handful of enthusiastic implementers who soon tire of holding up the heavy load. Therefore, administrators and coaches need to have a plan for providing differentiated coaching in order to ensure continuity, coherence, and stability.

Teachers can choose from several options as they begin the coaching process. Either the teacher or the coach can volunteer to do one of the following.

- Model a strategy with the teachers' students to reassure the hesitant teachers that the strategy works.
- Plan lessons and co-teach with the teachers who initially needed support.
- Observe and give feedback to the teachers who are more secure, focusing on strengths and setting goals for the next observation.
- Identify a teacher who is willing to invite another to observe as the coach conducts an observation and coaching session.
- Show a video to a small group of teachers and role-play, giving feedback (in a positive, supportive way, of course).

Coaches Reflect on Data to Adjust Course

Self-reflection and adjustment based on collected data is a critical component in the differentiated coaching process. K. Hamner, the professional development coordinator for Shelby County Schools in Memphis, Tennessee, for example, brings school coaches together once a month and asks them to reflect on the progress of their caseload and trajectory of their learning. Coaches come together at the district level to consider adjusting the support they are giving and the time they spend with teachers and to analyze current outcomes and data.

The following series of questions spark reflection and adjustments to the service a coach provides throughout the process.

General considerations:

- How long have you been supporting each teacher on your caseload?
- Have teachers met their original goals? How do you know; what data and tools did you use?
- Did you create additional goals? What was the purpose of adding goals?
- Are teachers making progress toward those goals?

- What type of coaching support (modeling, co-planning, and such) have you provided the teachers or small groups? What were the outcomes?

Time allocations:

- How often are you coaching the teachers each week or month?
- Do you need to adjust the time spent with teachers who are not making progress?
- Do you need to try other coaching strategies with the teachers on your caseload?
- Can you decrease the amount of time you are spending with any teachers on your caseload? (Do you see evidence of building capacity?)

School support and communication:

- Have you communicated with the principal the progress or lack of progress to assist you in making decisions for future support?
- How has the school supported you in your work with the teachers?
- Does the school have a systematic plan for helping the range of teachers with EL strategies?

Adjustments to your support:

- Do your teachers show the capacity to attend professional development sessions, implement instructional practices, self-reflect, and seek out support when needed?
- Considering the time of the year, are you contemplating rolling anyone off your caseload? Why or why not?

TLC or PLC support:

- How many teams do you support?
- How long have you supported each group?
- How often do you meet with each?
- Do you need to adjust coaching support for these groups?

- Does the small group show capacity to move forward with the work without support?

Based on the previous questions, coaches should use a worksheet like the one in figure 5.2 to consider things they should be proud of and celebrate, as well as the changes they need to make and how to go about those.

I should celebrate . . .	I need to share with . . .	I will communicate by . . .
Changes I need to make	Steps to prepare	Support I need to communicate

Figure 5.2: Charting coaching progress.

*Visit **go.SolutionTree.com/EL** for a free reproducible version of this figure.*

Coaches and Principals Plan for Adjustments

After self-reflecting and analyzing observational and student data, schedule a meeting with the principal to adjust as necessary and to celebrate progress. For example, when a teacher asks the coach to observe her as she conducts the 7 Steps vocabulary, the coach can use the form in figure 5.2 to reflect on how the coaching experience went. First, it is important to celebrate the things that went well in that session. If some of it did not go well, perhaps the coach will want to communicate or share the experience with the principal or another coach. Afterward, the coach can write down changes and new steps to take to continue support into the future.

Peer Observations or Coaching

As a member of your school's TLC, you have a wonderful resource available to you: your teachers, instructional support staff members, and fellow administrators. Their combined years of experience most likely will number in the hundreds. This makes them excellent resources for observation of your own practices. Teachers frequently use peer observations, but they should also serve as a resource for professional growth—even when done by an administrator or supervisor. Formal and informal observations help teachers have an additional pair of eyes or an alternate viewpoint.

A Key Recommendation

During a peer observation, the teacher decides what is to be observed: the student behavior, student output, or an instructional strategy.

The same observation protocol can be used for peer and coaches' observations. The teachers decide what their observer should watch for: student behavior, student output, or an instructional strategy. Peer observations and coaching are collaborative in nature and are for the improvement and refining of a teacher's skills, *not* evaluative. Since they are not evaluative, they should not become a part of the teacher's file unless a teacher explicitly requests it for professional development plans or other professional growth.

Observation Versus Evaluation

Observation is the action of watching someone or something carefully in order to gain information. A few related words are *watching, considering, reviewing,* and *collecting data.* Evaluation is making a judgment or assessment of value. The purpose of observation is to gather data and information. An evaluation is also for gathering data and information, but it has a deeper purpose of formulating an assessment about what the observer sees.

As you can see, the words *observation* and *evaluation* are not synonyms. Many times, administrators find it hard to separate the two. One North Carolina middle school administrator used to remind himself and his teachers of the difference with a physical signal. He bought

several caps that said coach on the front. The caps
were accompanied by an additional reminder of the
roles and duties of an effective coach neatly typed on
a card attached to a lanyard. The principal even wore
the cap and lanyard when doing coaching walks with
his staff. This helped teachers understand and have frank
discussions about the differences when they themselves
did peer observations.

Peer observers and coaches can conduct their observations in a
variety of ways. Ask your rock-star teachers to be open to having
other teachers observe them and then reciprocate. Eventually, any
teacher will be open to visiting any other teacher. This comes with
a great deal of trust and takes time to cultivate, but the benefits
are worth the time and energy. Core content teachers can observe
electives or enrichment teachers (computer science, art, and so on).
Mathematics teachers can observe social studies teachers; lower-
grade teachers can observe upper-grade teachers—there's no end to
the possibilities. Some districts even facilitate teachers visiting and
observing teachers in other buildings.

If you have stellar teachers who are willing to be videotaped, have
them record themselves or provide help to have them recorded.
Coaches can use these clips as examples of how to implement the
targeted professional development. This is a great way to show future
teachers or those who want to review the schools' expectations.

Self-reflection is another great tool for improvement. Teachers
can video themselves and use the observation protocol for their
reflections. There are a number of ways to do a quick video: with
an iPhone, iPad, webcam, or product such as a Swivl, which is specifically designed for short videos. Regardless of the method, make
sure that you have a video release form on file for any students who
you record, and that you have alternate plans for those who decline.

Conclusion

Coaching is a powerful tool for ensuring a proper implementation of knowledge and skills that teachers attain at a workshop
or at a comprehensive institute. Nonetheless, coaches need support themselves. If they are to coach teachers who begin to practice
instructional strategies focusing on ELs and all students in their
classrooms, the coach needs to attend the same training as the

teachers. We have found that the typical type of coaching model mainstream coaches use, or the coaching checklists, do not take into consideration instruction for ELs. This is why coaches need an additional day after the professional development with the teachers to learn what to look for and how to help the teacher be reflective and plan next steps.

Coaches need their own support system as they often need to communicate with someone about issues that might arise. This may be another coach or the principal or an expert coach who provided the training. We applaud Shelby County central district for bringing all coaches together once a month to share successes, debrief, problem solve, and learn more about coaching.

Just as coaches need continual learning and sharing with peers to fine-tune their craft, so do principals, assistant principals, and site coordinators. The next chapter describes the role of the principal in language minority schools and the type of professional development that helps them lead the way to effective change.

Discussion Questions

Consider the following.

- How will you present the idea of a comprehensive coaching program to the whole school?
- What aspects of coaching do you need to highlight to mitigate the thinking that these visits might be evaluative?
- What percentage of your professional development funds go to expert coaching? Peer coaching? Substitutes to enable any type of coaching?
- What do you need to do to design and implement a two-year plan?

CHAPTER 6

Sustaining a Quality Implementation

Systematic implementation

Academic definition: A methodical procedure to execute a plan or decision

Friendly definition: Taking regular action according to a plan

---

As part of our trainings of teachers, administrators, superintendents, and other support staff, we change roles from presenters and trainers to classroom coaches and observers. When we have the wonderful privilege of visiting schools and classrooms across the United States, we have the joy of seeing multiple varied implementations of the strategies we present. On one such visit, in the spring of 2016 in Tennessee, we were impressed with an elementary school staff that was well on their way toward whole-school implementation of ExC-ELL.

Teachers who attended our session returned to their school and, while practicing their new skills, shared with two colleagues who were absent the day of the professional development. This fact came to our attention after observing the 7 Steps vocabulary strategy in a mathematics lesson. It came out in casual conversation that the teacher we had just observed, having done a phenomenal job, had not actually attended the session. Upon further discussion with this teacher, we found that the principal, who did attend the sessions with her staff, expected that all those who attended professional development sessions share what they learned with those who could not attend.

As part of our administrator training on coaching and supporting teachers, the principal shadowed us while we observed and coached her teachers. Her staff informed us that she regularly helped find coverage and time for her teachers to meet and plan together or visit each other's classrooms. It became quite evident that the leader of this school had high expectations, expressed them to her staff, and felt it was her duty to learn with her school.

This example of how to implement expectations and provide support can and should be implemented in any school that seeks to implement effective whole-school strategies. Administration and leadership must lead the way in inspecting and supporting this expectation, which includes, but is not limited to, attending all professional development training with the staff. Over the course of this chapter we'll explore some of the qualities required of successful leaders and how they can set expectations, implement successful processes, and provide the feedback necessary for real growth.

Shared Leadership

Much of your time as a leader will not be out front in the lead. Good leaders are with the team listening, learning, modeling, and setting expectations. In a school, as the leader, all eyes are on you. This is nothing new, but it is worth reiterating. So let's connect shared leadership with the focus on ELs.

Leaders who listen know who to listen to and who not to listen to (Senge et al., 2012). Sometimes that means you have to listen to yourself and ask:

- How do you communicate with your teachers, the students, ELs' parents, and the community?
- When was the last time you listened to one of your ELs?

Sometimes, listening means not responding, waiting to let others work out the problem or come up with the solution. Other times, it involves listening to your ELs about what they are learning and how they are learning it.

Leaders are learners. Principals learn with their staffs. They make time to learn and look for new experiences. As the leader of a learning institution, ask yourself these questions.

- What have you learned lately?
- What can you learn from your staff?
- What have you learned by just listening in PLCs and TLCs?
- What have you learned from or for your ELs recently?

Leaders are comfortable strategically sharing the leadership. Managers tell people to do things. Good leaders find those who are excellent at what they do, have those rock stars share what they know, and learn from them. Great leaders share the responsibility, use the skills and resources available to them, and know their limitations. They aren't afraid to say "I don't know, but I'll get back to you" or "Let's find the answers together" (Kouzes & Posner, 2012; Senge et al., 2012).

Leaders are consistent, sincere, and persistent. Great leaders mean what they say and say what they mean. In the end, this saves time and energy. They also endure because they aren't afraid to fail; rather, they see failure as a way to learn how to do it better next time. Maybe with some help.

Expect that you can't do it all. Expect that you must have the help and support of teachers. Expect that your teachers *will* help. Work with them to be a successful community with a focused, clearly defined culture of teaching, learning, and ongoing professional development and purpose (Knight, 2011).

Message Expectations for the Transfer From Training to Classroom Instruction

Leadership through support and guidance has many facets. In previous chapters, we've discussed the framework of professional development, observations, and learning communities of which a critical and complex facet of supporting teachers and classroom instruction is messaging expectations. A common saying in many supervisory circles is that you must *inspect the expectation*. The expectation needs a clear and concise description, plan of implementation, and method of determining attainment.

Just as teachers must have a lesson plan for students, those who coach and support, or even evaluate, must also have a plan. What are the components of that plan? What message or messages about

EL achievement do you have in mind? What do you expect to see as evidence of meeting the expectation?

This process requires your involvement before, during, and after training.

Before the Professional Development Session: Messaging and Planning

The goal of professional development is to advance a teacher's skill set and ensure that students are successful at the end of the year. Each teacher who attends a professional development session should know from the start that he or she is expected to use the newly acquired knowledge in his or her daily practice. As an administrator, supervisor, or coach, you too must attend the professional development session with the same thought in mind. Consider the following questions.

- Which components will you need to see when you return to observe the implementation in the classroom? These components will be the basis for your observations from then on.
- Who will be assisting you in developing and checking in on the plan?
- How will you share the success of the implementation or the need for its refinement?

This process begins by simply sending an email or a note letting your teachers know that you look forward to attending the training with them. Ask if there is anything they need from you to help them get the most out of the session, or ask them what they expect to get out of the session. This in and of itself sends a very clear message—you value this training. It also communicates that you know of what you speak when you observe or coach your teachers after the session. Kouzes and Posner (2012) allude to this in their First Law of Leadership: "If we don't believe in the messenger, we won't believe the message" (p. 26). If teachers don't believe that you have the background to coach and help, they won't value your guidance.

Follow up on the responses to your requests for help in getting the most out of the training. Even more important is to follow up with those who don't respond. Find out why they haven't responded. You are expecting all to attend, participate, and then implement. Give it the personal touch—go in person to make sure that the teachers got your message and to see what they expect to get from the training. What obstacles might they have in attending and fully participating? Be ready yourself with what you expect to get out of it for your personal and professional growth. Yes, this might be awkward for some and not your style, but look at it as checking in on your investment, both of the teacher and the funds you're expending on professional development.

During the Professional Development Session

Here is where it sometimes gets sticky. Remember the trite—but true—saying, "Actions speak louder than words"? As an administrator, you have many responsibilities. However, when you are at the professional development session, your primary focus is what you and your teachers are learning. If you don't have an idea of what the training involves, how can you reliably determine and support your teachers after the training? So here's the difficult part: put away the cell phone, close the email account, and be fully present for the training. You would not be there that day if you didn't have the confidence that those you left in charge could handle your school without you. When you delegate, you not only help others to grow, but you show that you are paying attention to all aspects of your job (Senge et al., 2012).

Most of all, enjoy the training. This is your professional development opportunity, too. Take notes; discuss the new information with your team; share your views on what teachers should transfer to all the classrooms. You are sitting with one of the teams, aren't you? Move from team to team throughout the session. You might want to ask questions such as the following.

- "Who would like to volunteer to lead a TLC centered around these new strategies?"
- "Who would like to share what those who were unable to attend missed?"
- "What parts of the session do your teachers need more information about?"
- "What supplies might they need?"
- "Whose commitment do I have to help infuse these into the entire school's instructional repertoire?"

By the end of the session, you'll have a good idea of the first steps you would like to see in the classroom the next time you visit. You will have connected with those teachers you know you can count on to help promote the use of these new skills.

Before You Leave the Training

Before leaving the training, take a few minutes to make some implementation and expectation notes. The following questions will help spark the next part of your planning process.

- What did you *all* agree you should infuse into the instruction at your school based on this professional development session?
- What are the first steps?
- What more do your teachers need to be successful in transferring these new skills into the classroom?
- Who has agreed to help and how?
- If the session is several days long, do you know what you and your teachers need to bring to the next session?
- Do you yourself need more clarification on certain pieces? Who can you go to? One of your fellow participants?
- Do you have the contact information for the professional development trainer so you can ask for clarification on the items presented?
- Have you planned and communicated when this process will start?

Answering these questions will help focus what you've learned and help you design the beginning of a whole-school implementation plan.

After the Professional Development Session: Setting the Tone at School

On the next day back or even the night after the training, email those who participated in the training, and thank them for their time and energy. Share one or two things you enjoyed from the session. Ask them to share what they liked or how they plan to proceed. Encourage them to invite others who may have experience, expertise, or desire to be a part of formulating and rolling out the plan.

Later in the week or the start of the following week, communicate with your fellow attendees where and when all of you will be meeting to debrief the professional development session and plan your next steps. Send a reminder; include the expectation that all should attend. Let them know you'd like them to bring the materials provided for the training. Invite them to bring what they have already started themselves. More likely than not, at least one person has already had some success with the new skills. If someone volunteered to share or start the process, recognize that person. You should lead the discussion. You are there to set the expectation that the skills be implemented and to be a resource for assisting in that implementation.

If possible, treat attendees when they get there. It doesn't have to be a three-course meal. Chocolate or sweets or even something as simple as a soda or bottle of water is sufficient. As we will discuss later in this chapter, celebrate any successes that your teachers have already had. Perhaps you've already seen the skills in use while you are doing your instructional walkthroughs. Share those successes and give credit to those implementing their newfound knowledge.

If you have gotten this far, congratulations! You are on your way to having a TLC. But before your TLC concludes their meeting, be sure to have established meeting norms for respectful collaboration, a consensus on the next steps to implementation, and an understanding that transfer to the classroom is the expected goal. Make expectations and accountability clear. If you need some help getting started, use the checklist in figure 6.1 to help get yourself organized.

☐ Reminder of Professional Development Session
  • Provide date, time, and location.
  • Attend to registration, obtaining a substitute, and so on.
  • Note expectations for follow-up upon return.
  • Check for needs to attend to.
  • Let them know you'll be there, too.
☐ Attendee Follow-Up
  • Check on those who agreed to attend.
  • Did you invite substitutes?
  • Do attendees have other needs to get the most out of the session?

☐ Day of Professional Development Planning
   • Sit with your team or teams.
   • Be there at the training! Turn off cell phone and participate. No emails, either.
   • Get commitments on who will be helping with post professional development implementation.
☐ After the Training
   • Email attendees, thank them for attending, and share your take-ways.
   • Invite them to share their thoughts, as well.
   • Remind them of where and when the debriefing session will be held.
   • Plan what treat you'll bring.
   • Remind them to bring their supplies and successes.
☐ Implementation Message
   • Tell them what you'll be looking for and when.
   • Determine how you will collect data and provide feedback.
   • Ask teachers to invite you at a good time.
   • Be there.
   • Share the good things you saw.
☐ Repeat With Next Expectation
   • Tell them what you'll be looking for and when. What are the next steps?
   • How will you collect data and provide feedback?
   • Ask teachers to invite you at a good time.
   • Share who will be coming with you.
   • Be there.
   • Share the good things you saw.
☐ Celebrate and Share

Figure 6.1: Messaging checklist (written, oral, and subliminal).

*Visit **go.SolutionTree.com/EL** for a free reproducible version of this figure.*

The professional development session was most likely rigorous and detailed, with many components. When communicating what you expect upon its completion, start small. Most strategies take time to develop, time to teach the structure to the students, plus time to reflect, review, and refine. So start with a simple expectation and give your teachers ample time to prepare. If you have a Friday memo or a communication system in place for staff-related announcements, use it to let your staff know what you'll be looking for. For instance, "Folks, in my walkthroughs next week, I'd like to see those of you who attended the ExC-ELL training doing the 7 Steps for preteaching vocabulary for at least two words. If you tell me a specific time you'll be doing this with your class, I'll do my best to be there."

Monday Memo

From: Mike_St_Claire@anyschool.net
To: ExC-ELL Institute Participants
Subject: Walk-through looks fors

Folks, in my walk-throughs next week, I'd like to see those of you who attended the ExC-ELL training doing the 7 Steps for preteaching vocabulary for a least two words. If you tell me a specific time you'll be doing this with your class, I'll do my best to be there.

Mike

Be specific in your expectations. Remind teachers again at the beginning of the week. Then keep your promise, and go looking. When you see evidence of someone beginning to use the strategy, make sure the teacher knows you saw what you were looking to see.

When you're done with your walkthroughs, share the successes you saw with everyone. Remember, you aren't looking for perfection, just evidence that the process is starting. When you see someone doing an exceptionally good job, ask them if you can send others to see their success and progress, or ask if they would be willing to be a resource for others.

Higher Expectation Levels

After you've shared what you saw, it is time to raise the level of expectation. Move on to the next component or increase the rigor. Remember to clearly communicate what you expect to see. For example, "Colleagues, I saw several great beginnings with our new strategies this week. Ms. Jackson's and Mr. Del Toro's classes are progressing nicely with the 7 Steps. If you have questions, they've agreed to help out. Remember, preteaching vocabulary needs to happen with every lesson, so this week's goal is to use the 7 Steps in at least two subjects or increase the number of words you teach to at least four or five. I'll be looking at that all-important step 6 of 100 percent student engagement. See you next week."

Continue building step by step, component by component. Celebrate the successes; recognize the parts that teachers need to revisit. Be consistent, vigilant, and reasonable—you're looking for implementation and fidelity, not rigidity.

As part of your messaging, let the teachers know how they will get feedback, how you will be taking notes, when you will share, and what data you will be collecting, both for refinement and celebration. Let the teachers know, "Friends, in our walkthroughs we'll be using the Reading Comprehension piece of the WISEcard. I'm just seeing which pieces the ELs are doing well and in which subjects. I'll bring my notes to the next TLC meeting. Keep up the great teaching!"

Continue to support your TLC. Most TLCs fizzle out due to lack of administrator support. You don't have to attend every meeting. Sometimes it is a good idea to not attend a meeting now and then. Doing so gives your teachers time to support each other. If you say you will be there, then fully be there. There will be those days or times when you aren't or can't be there. As a fail-safe you can refer to the meeting notes that were part of the norms you first established. All members get a copy of the meeting notes even if—and maybe especially if—they missed a TLC meeting. Have and communicate expectations for each meeting.

Communicating

Who else do you need to communicate with about the professional development session and new knowledge? Have you let your students' parents know? They deserve to know that your teachers are learning new things that will benefit their children. Perhaps this communication needs to be part of the implementation plan that the TLC develops. Your students' parents can't help if they don't know how they can support their children's learning. Inform them of the expectations for the teachers, students, school, and yourself. Let them know also how teachers will assess expectations, share successes, and plan adjustments.

What about your supervisors? Your administrator colleagues? Absolutely! Invite them to come and see your successes for themselves. While you're at it, have you communicated with the trainer who facilitated the training or the department that provided or paid for the professional development session? Do you have suggestions? Questions? Were other teachers and administrators outside your building in attendance, too? What successes and encouragement can you share?

Coaching and Coaches

Are coaching and peer observations part of the expectation? Are your instructional coaches included in your expectations? Go with your coaches during their teacher observations. How do they focus on ELs? What are some questions they might still have? What type of feedback are they giving the teachers?

One way to check in on progress is by doing a walkthrough. Another way is to celebrate!

Walkthroughs

Walkthroughs, Learning Walks, Three-Minute Visits, Snapshots—the name changes, but the intent should not. Take them! The Japanese custom of Hanami (花見) is a stroll or picnic for the enjoyment of the spring flowers, typically the cherry blossoms. As an administrator, you probably don't have time for many strolls through your school, but the sentiment is the same. Make it a custom to enjoy the teaching and learning that is blossoming in your school. You have invested a great deal of time, talent, money, and human capital. While taking your walkthroughs, you will see how your school is flourishing. When you set the tone, your teachers are ready. Invite others to go with you. Explain to your teachers that talking with the students is not meant to interrupt their instruction but rather to ask the students what they are learning and how the strategies are helping them. Your students will give you some of the best data you will ever get.

Be upbeat. Be consistent. Remain focused. When distractions come up, make a note of what you need to deal with later and keep going. Let your staff and fellow administrators know that you are booked for this time and will be happy to help them when you are done.

Have a plan for your route. Start at the back of the school one day. The next time start at the other end. Take some walks in the morning and others in the afternoon. One administrator in New York City Schools had a special pair of shoes that he showed to the staff at a meeting at the end of the year when they were celebrating the students' growth in mathematics and reading (T. Chan, personal communication, August 24, 2014). He had completely worn them out! He was proud that he had visited every classroom many, many times and saw every teacher practicing the new strategies they had all learned. Now that's inspecting the expectation.

Celebrate!

Celebrating successes, no matter how small, is an integral part of an effective implementation and messaging plan. Something as simple as a note to a teacher that implemented a component of the training will send a louder message than anything you can send in an email or announcement. Achievements of benchmarks must be part of the messaging plan and process. Recognize that you saw what you were looking for and that you are proud of what is happening at your school and in your classrooms. Celebrate after critical benchmark assessments. Invite parents of ELs to celebrations. They will become your allies and friends with these invitations. They are also anxious to know how their children are progressing. Regardless of the language they speak, they will readily understand *a spirit of celebration*. As your whole-school endeavor continues, you will see from the data analysis that there will be many good things to celebrate.

An ExC-ELLent Classroom in Action

In a second-grade classroom at Kate Bond Elementary in Shelby, Tennessee, the students sat in teams of four, ready to hear their teachers' instructions (A. Garland, S. Kuhn, & K. Kersey, personal communication, March 15, 2016). One was an ESL teacher; the other, the general education teacher. It was difficult to tell which was which since they took turns conducting the whole lesson. One explained that each team would write one question based on the text they had just read with their partner. Each team would receive a card with one of the levels from Bloom's taxonomy. They were to create a question and the answer and then write the question on the front and the answer on the back of the provided index card. Additionally, they were to use certain academic words in their questions and answers. Instead of *said*, they were to use the new words they had just read, words of *specificity* for their particular focus. For this reason, the other teacher had pretaught these words and had written them on a chart as reminders.

Just as the teacher said, "You have ten minutes to do this," the lights went out in the school.

This did not bother the students. They were busy discussing, revisiting the text, and drafting questions. When the teachers' peer coach noticed that the students couldn't see the chart tablet, he used his iPhone as a flashlight. As a result, the students completed everything within the ten minutes, and each team submitted quality questions written in correct academic English.

After students finished the question-writing task, the teachers used a cooperative learning strategy called Numbered Heads Together for the teams to read their question and have ample discussions, deliberations, and a few polite rounds of argumentative discourse that took them deeper into the text.

Using the Numbered Heads Together Strategy

Numbered Heads Together is a strategy that encourages all students to answer. It provides the teacher with a systematic process to ensure all students participate by assigning each student a number. A question is read, all students discuss the answer within their small groups—making sure all group members have the answer, then the teacher calls a number between one and four. If for example, the teacher calls out number three, all those students who have that number are required to stand and work through the process of answering the question. A process of polite discourse using starters such as *I agree with*, *I disagree with*, and *I'd like to add* . . . are used to provide respectful discourse. The activity continues until all students have participated.

Later, eight exemplary teachers from Kate Bond Elementary came up with the idea to present and share tools such as these with the new cohort of eighty teachers from other schools. The eight are on their way to becoming trainers of trainers.

Conclusion

Inspecting the expectation is only the beginning. For whole-school implementation, all members of the school play an active part and are accountable. Administrators, coaches, teachers, and students alike need to understand the expectation and how it will be assessed, recorded, recognized, and, when needed, refined. The staff's expectation for the administration may be unwritten, but every person the principal, assistant principal, or support staff supports or evaluates will be thinking, "By what authority do they speak?" or "How am I supposed to know that is what they want if they don't tell me?" So tell them clearly and show them by your actions that you are there with them as part of the team.

Discussion Questions

Consider the following.

- What messages do you give before a professional development training session? Expectations? During professional development training? Right after professional development training?
- What messages do you give about coaching? About the difference between coaching and evaluation?
- How do you celebrate with your staff, and how often?

CHAPTER 7

Whole-School Approach to Success for ELs (and All Other Students)

Whole

Academic definition: Comprising the full quantity, amount, extent, number, and such without diminution or exception; entire, full, or total

Friendly definition: Including everybody

Who is responsible for the academic success of ELs? By this point in the book, you know that that answer to this question is *everyone in the school!* Every time we offer our ExC-ELL institutes, we hear teachers say, "ELs are not the only students who need to learn and apply academic language—all our students do!" "Many of our Title I students come from homes where low-quality English is spoken or rarely spoken because parents are not home." "These strategies work for all our students. This year, the SAT scores went up exponentially because we all taught vocabulary."

Whole-school approaches to teaching vocabulary, reading comprehension, and writing as described throughout this book are now a trend that benefits all students. All teachers in a school are retooling to be able to teach academic vocabulary, reading comprehension, and writing in a way that helps the ELs in their classrooms, be they few or many. Interestingly, teachers find that it helps their low-level readers as well as the students in their advanced placement classrooms. In fact, we have been training entire school staffs, teachers, and administrators in schools with only one or no ELs. Upon hearing about the approach, they realized that this would help their entire student body. While working in Massachusetts on a similar project, we realized that even though we were initially helping teachers work with the state's seventy-four thousand ELs, those teachers who received the sheltered English instruction endorsement training and implemented those strategies in their classrooms helped to provide improved instruction to more than a million students each year. Yes, schools with high populations of ELs are the ones most likely to see benefits they had never seen before, but it doesn't have to stop there.

In this chapter we take a look at the broad range of benefits inherent in a whole-school approach to supporting EL students as well as some myths regarding whole-school implementation.

Benefits of the Whole-School Approach

Regardless of the composition of the student population or the bilingual, ESL, or sheltered English instruction program, schools that implement the training and follow-up coaching found in this book, as a whole-school effort, find many benefits.

- Everyone has a chance to catch up on the latest research, knowledge, and practices for ELs. Everyone is on the same page. This becomes an equalizer, because not all teachers have the whole spectrum of teaching, from selecting words to teach to the very end where students are producing quality writing.
- Everyone is trying something new at the same time. They are more prone to empathize and support one another.
- Funding goes further. Instead of hiring various consultants for multiple groups, the same consultants serve the whole school.
- Coaching schedules become easier. More teachers are available on any given day.

- All teachers in the school relate better to ELs and appreciate their strengths and efforts.
- Best, there is a shared language and more collaboration among teachers, coaches, and administrators.

The shift from one ESL teacher dealing with sixty ELs to a whole school genuinely concerned with sixty ELs and revamping their teaching skills to ensure success is not easy! Less easy is a school with 20 percent or more of ELs. Sometimes, the larger the population of ELs, the more difficult it becomes to bring change. Some schools that have been dealing with ELs for long periods of time find it more difficult to change due to long standing myths about ELs and their instruction.

Myths Regarding Whole-School Implementation

One of the more certain ways to doom a whole-school approach to supporting ELs is to fail to overcome preconceived notions about the work involved in achieving success. Certain myths can derail or reinforce inertia, and it's your job to overcome those myths right from the start. For example, here are some we often hear, along with answers you can adapt to counter them.

- "We only need an hour of professional development on vocabulary."
  Selecting and teaching vocabulary, artfully integrated into all content areas, requires at least six hours of professional development and three to five days of coaching to go from the declarative to procedural to conditional knowledge and efficacy.
- "An ESL teacher will take care of all our ELs' needs."
  One or more ESL teachers cannot address all the academic language that ELs need to learn in mathematics, science, social studies, electives, and language arts. In addition, ELs need content-based academic language instruction. ESL teachers are charged with teaching ELs the foundations and rudiments of English, not content.

- "All certified ESL teachers are well prepared and highly qualified to teach ELs."

  Some ESL, ELD, and sheltered English instruction teachers earned their credentials many years ago in programs that did not teach recent research-based, evidence-based methods for the complete integration of vocabulary, reading comprehension, and writing. These teachers, as with all teachers, require up-to-date professional development to maintain their understanding of the best learning strategies and practices.

- "Our teachers teach vocabulary throughout the day already."

  But is their teaching reaching? What methods are they using? Do they take half a period to teach one or two words? What connections with vocabulary are directly and explicitly connected to reading comprehension and writing?

- "It takes ELs seven to ten years to become proficient, anyway."

  That was true five or ten years ago, or even today when instruction is questionable. The only reason this has ever been true is in cases where programs lacked rigor. Students did not develop academic language and reading comprehension skills, which impacted negatively on writing and content learning. It becomes a self-fulfilling prophecy that results in why the country's EL population consists of 70–80 percent long-term ELs. (Calderón & Minaya-Rowe, 2011)

- "We have to wait for them to come out of their *silent period*."

  With respect to our colleagues who posit this theory, it is only that—a theory. No empirical research supports this thinking. In our experience, when students are caringly induced to speak—even on the first day of entering your school—they will indeed speak and begin the learning process. This also sets the tone of expectation: learning starts now.

- "The parents of ELs don't care about their education." Language minority parents are *parents*. They care about their children's education. The reason they came to this country was to give their children a better education and promise for a better life. When schools do not reach out in their language, they feel uninvited. Moreover, it is incumbent upon the school and district to teach the parents about their and their children's educational rights—that they as parents have the right to be fully involved and informed. In fact, it is expected.

- "Teaching in two languages hampers English development."

  Dual-language programs develop English and the partner language at high levels (Collier & Thomas, 2004; Valdes, 1997). However, these programs need to be extremely well structured so that both languages are developed at grade-level each year.

- "Mathematics, science, social studies, and language arts teachers do not have time to teach language; they need to cover their subjects."

  On day one of our professional development, we always hear, "I don't have time to teach vocabulary. I need to cover my curriculum." "I have to keep up with my pacing guide." "I am not a reading teacher. I teach biology."

  Then, by day three, the same teachers say, "Why didn't anyone teach me this before?" "This is going to be so easy." "Can I use this in every class?" "Yes, I am a reading teacher—and a language teacher too!"

There is always opposition to change, and introducing new, more effective practices to support ELs presents both change and challenge to teachers who already face change and challenge on a daily basis. Knowing myths about the whole-school approach to supporting ELs and arming yourself with facts that can overcome pushback will help you instill a call to action in your educators that effects real change.

A Call to Action

The only way to create change in mindsets (the kind of mindsets that result in the myths we just discussed), particularly in schools with large percentages of ELs, is to do a whole-school comprehensive professional development with a well-supported, communicated, examined, reviewed, and coached process of follow-through, as we have described here. Piecemeal or watered-down approaches do not change mindsets and certainly can't overcome obsolete instructional practices. All educators in a school are responsible for the success of all students. Are your educators being held accountable?

In order for schools to catch up with demographic change and challenges from the federal and state governments, the whole-school approach is the only recourse. As we showed you in chapter 6, the principal's messages will sustain the momentum and commitment by all the teachers. Fullan (2002) states that, "Only principals who are equipped to handle a complex, rapidly changing environment can implement the reforms that lead to sustained improvement in student achievement" (p. 16).

The continual development of leadership talent is fast becoming an imperative (Hill, 2005), particularly for the leadership in schools with growing numbers of ELs. In addition to administrators' academies or specific professional development, coaching or mentoring principals has become a trend. School districts assign mentors to new principals. When the state takes over a low-performing school, it assigns the principal a mentor. Some districts have established a leadership coaching department composed of former teachers with coaching or administration experience to support school leaders in their development and in school improvement (Aguilar, Goldwasser, & Tank-Crestetto, 2011).

Whereas teachers can significantly influence student learning with their instructional practices, principals are equally influential in increasing student learning. Coaching for school leaders is vital to develop not only individual leadership capacity but systems leaders. Effective educational leaders create environments that foster capacity development and reinforce and sustain ongoing learning (Devine, Meyers, & Houssemand, 2013).

Notwithstanding the additional resource, mentors and principals don't always sync well in terms of philosophy or expertise. The chasm is created when the mentor does not have the same knowledge about ELs as the school's teachers and leadership. If the mentor or coach does not attend the professional development with the mentee and school staff, the effort becomes moot. We experienced such a conundrum in an elementary school where the principal and teachers were going through a comprehensive professional development on the twelve components of EL instruction. The principal's mentor had very little knowledge (mainly obsolete theories and some myths about ELs) but still felt she should impose her philosophy and practice. After a few weeks, the mentor swayed the principal into doing things the mentor's way. That kept the status quo and kept the mentor happy; a requirement since the mentor was evaluating the principal. The mentor's way did nothing to benefit EL students and thus the ELs in the end lost out on strategies that would have benefited them.

So what is the answer to all this? Get everyone involved in the professional development and coaching! It is the only way to sustain the effort long enough to see excellent results for ELs and all students and to retain an enthusiastic, highly skilled and fulfilled teaching corps. In figure 7.1, we provide an implementation rubric to help you along the way.

A. Identifying and Assessing All Potential EL Students

Strong Implementation	Where we are:	What we need to do:
1. School or district has a process to identify ELs accurately and in a timely fashion. Teachers and administrators know this process and act accordingly.		
2. School or district determines whether potential EL students are in fact EL through a valid and reliable test that assesses English language proficiency in speaking, listening, reading, and writing. Teachers and administrators know which students are highly schooled newcomers, unaccompanied minors, homeless ELs, long-term ELs, students with interrupted formal education, special education ELs, and reclassified ELs.		

Figure 7.1: Rubric for implementation.   continued ⇨

B. Staffing and Providing Language Assistance to EL Students

Strong Implementation	Where we are:	What we need to do:
1. Appropriate ELD or ESL services provided for ELs at different levels of listening, speaking, reading, and writing proficiency and background factors (unaccompanied newcomers, highly schooled newcomers, long-term ELs, and so on).		
2. All core content, electives, bilingual, special education, and specialty teachers use exemplary practices for integrating language, literacy, and content (for example, ExC-ELL).		
3. All core content, ELD, ESL, sheltered English instruction, bilingual, and special education teachers base their lessons on language standards.		
4. All teachers are qualified to teach ELs, and administrators are qualified to lead the school toward an EL-successful implementation.		
5. School has highly qualified ESL, ELD, and core content teachers and support personnel prepared to address educational needs of ELs.		
6. Administrators and teachers of core content, specialties, and electives continually attend professional development sessions to update their skills for integrating vocabulary, discourse, reading, and writing into their subject areas.		
7. School has established teams for teachers to share lessons, model strategies, and discuss EL progress. School provides supplemental training when necessary.		

C. Providing Meaningful Access to All Curricular and Extracurricular Programs

Strong Implementation	Where we are:	What we need to do:
1. ELs have access to grade-level curricula so that they can meet promotion and graduation requirements.		
2. ESL or ELD materials are age appropriate and address state standards.		
3. ELs participate in all programs: magnet, gifted and talented, career and technical education, arts, athletics, and advanced placement; International Baccalaureate courses; clubs; and honor societies.		

D. Avoiding Unnecessary Segregation of EL Students

Strong Implementation	Where we are:	What we need to do:
1. While receiving separate instruction for a limited portion of the day for targeted ESL, ELs have access to core content and curricular and extracurricular activities. (Typically level 1 and 2 students receive two hours of ESL, one and a half hours for level 3, and half an hour for levels 4 and 5 of ESL daily. Time varies by state. ELs should spend the remainder of the day in core content and extracurricular activities with mainstream students.)		

E. Evaluating EL Students for Special Education and Providing Dual Services

Strong Implementation	Where we are:	What we need to do:
1. Identify, locate, and evaluate ELs for special education in a timely manner.		
2. Provide EL students with disabilities both the language assistance and the disability-related services to which they are entitled under federal law.		
3. Evaluate ELs in an appropriate language-based assessment of their needs and language skills; the team designing their plan includes ESL or ELD personnel.		

continued ⇨

F. Monitoring and Exiting EL Students From EL Programs and Services

Strong Implementation	Where we are:	What we need to do:
1. Monitor exited ELs to ensure language proficiency and content knowledge within a reasonable time.		
2. Offer specialized courses and activities to help long-term ELs access grade-level core content.		
3. Offer compensatory services and differentiated intervention programs with after-school or Saturday activities to help ELs accelerate their learning.		
4. Monitor opt-out ELs for their progress and offer services if they are struggling.		

G. Ensuring Meaningful Communications With Limited English Proficient Parents

Strong Implementation	Where we are:	What we need to do:
1. Inform parents of their rights in a language they understand about the range of EL services that their child could receive and the benefits of such services.		
2. Translate all information into the family home languages, and provide interpreters as necessary.		

H. Evaluating the Effectiveness of a School's EL Program

Strong Implementation	Where we are:	What we need to do:
1. Evaluate EL program, services, and general classroom instruction using accurate data to assess the educational performance of current and former EL students and make timely modifications when needed.		
2. Evaluate the professional development program currently in place; evaluate the transfer from the training, and the frequency, fidelity, and quality of the implementation from the professional development. If it is not effective, it needs to be improved.		

Conclusion

Although success for all students is used as a goal in schools across the United States, there are very few schools that act on this mantra in the comprehensive way we mapped here. As the EL population continues to rise, as well as the number of non-ELs not reading at grade level, it behooves every school, district, and state in the country to espouse a whole-school approach that focuses on teaching academic language, reading comprehension (sometimes basic reading), and academic writing skills that are integrated into every subject. A whole-school approach also helps to meet the new ESSA and USDOJ accountability requirements. This book highlighted the vital pieces that bring everyone together for a common cause.

As leaders, you and your colleagues seek five-star quality on a daily basis. You entered the profession because you wanted to make a difference in education. You promised yourself, your students, and your colleagues that you would, to tweak the Hippocratic oath, lead or teach to the best of your ability. You aspire to create the school where all your students succeed and your teams excel. As a teacher leader or administrative leader, you are ready to begin that journey. That is why you are reading this (and probably other books) to guide you through the journey of change and excitement. Taking to heart the suggestions and guidelines we outlined in this book will help you along that path to fulfill those promises you made to your students, your colleagues, and most importantly to yourself.

Discussion Questions

Consider the following.

- What myths are still pervasive in your school?
- What benefits do you anticipate from a whole-school approach?
- How soon can you start your whole-school professional development?
- How long can your ELs afford to wait for you to start?

APPENDIX A

Recommended Books and Online Resources

In this appendix, we list some useful books and websites for you to use to extend your knowledge and understanding of serving ELs.

Recommended Books

Calderón, M. E. (2007). *Teaching reading to English language learners, grades 6–12: A framework for improving achievement in the content areas.* Thousand Oaks, CA: Corwin Press.

Calderón, M. E. (2011). *Preventing long-term ELs: Transforming schools to meet core standards.* Thousand Oaks, CA: Corwin Press.

Calderón, M. E. (2011). *Teaching reading & comprehension to English learners, K–5.* Bloomington, IN: Solution Tree Press.

Calderón, M. E. (2012). *Breaking through: Effective instruction & assessment for reaching English learners.* Bloomington, IN: Solution Tree Press.

Calderón, M. E., & Minaya-Rowe, L. (2003). *Designing and implementing two-way bilingual programs: A step-by-step guide for administrators, teachers, and parents.* Thousand Oaks, CA: Corwin Press.

Calderón, M. E., & Soto, I.. (2016). *Academic language mastery: Vocabulary in context.* Thousand Oaks, CA: Corwin Press.

Calderón, M. E., Trejo, M. N., & Montenegro, H. (2016). *Literacy strategies for English learners in core content secondary classrooms.* Bloomington, IN: Solution Tree Press.

Recommended Online Resources

Best Evidence Encyclopedia. (n.d.). Accessed at www.bestevidence.org on September 16, 2016.

Center for Applied Linguistics. (n.d.). *Briefs & digests.* Accessed at www.cal.org/resource-center/briefs-digests on May 18, 2016.

Colorín Colorado. (n.d.). *Teaching English language learners.* Accessed at www.colorincolorado.org/teaching-english-language-learners on May 18, 2016.

Reading Rockets. (n.d.). *Vocabulary.* Accessed at www.readingrockets.org/reading-topics/vocabulary on May 18, 2016.

Solution Tree Press. (n.d.). [Search results: *Calderon, M. E.*] Accessed at www.solution-tree.com/searchresults/?q=Margarita%20Calderon on September 16, 2016.

Solution Tree Press. (n.d.). [Search results: *English learner books and videos*]. Accessed at www.solution-tree.com/products/l/english-learners.html on September 16, 2016.

Solution Tree Press. (n.d.). [Search results: *Soluciones*]. Accessed at www.solution-tree.com/searchresults/?q=soluciones on September 16, 2016.

U.S. Department of Education. (2015). *Schools' civil rights obligations to English learner students and limited English proficient parents.* Accessed at www2.ed.gov/about/offices/list/ocr/ellresources.html on May 18, 2016.

U.S. Department of Justice, Civil Rights Division & U.S. Department of Education, Office for Civil Rights. (2015). [Dear colleague letter about education and Title VI of the Civil Rights Act of 1964]. Accessed at www2.ed.gov/about/offices/list/ocr/letters/colleague-el-201501.pdf on May 18, 2016.

U.S. Government Publishing Office. (2015). *Every Student Succeeds Act.* Accessed at www.gpo.gov/fdsys/pkg/BILLS-114s1177enr/pdf/BILLS-114s1177enr.pdf on September 16, 2016.

APPENDIX B
Glossary of EL Categories

This glossary lists some of the most common categories districts use to classify different types of EL students. Most of the language in these definitions comes from the U.S. Department of Justice and the U.S. Department of Education Guidelines' Dear Colleague Letters (USDOJ & USDOE, 2015b) and from the Every Student Succeeds Act ([ESSA], 2016).

English Learner Terms

EL: English learner. A shortened version of ELL and frequently used in the profession and throughout this book to refer to students who are learning English as an additional language.

ELL: English language learner. See **EL**.

FLEP: formerly limited English proficient. Students who have exited from official LEP status via a recognized assessment such as WIDA's ACCESS for ELLs. Prior to the Every Student Succeeds Act guidelines, FLEP students were to be monitored for a minimum of two years after exiting LEP status; however, ESSA guidelines now call for four years of monitoring. Some states may also refer to these students as MFLEP, adding the word *monitored*. No official change to this notation has evolved yet, so exited EL students are still referred to as FLEP.

HSN: highly schooled newcomers or ELs. Students who have a high degree of literacy or education in their native language and home. Frequently they have had years of English as a foreign language (EFL), and may be at or above the grade level of their never-EL peers, but need explicit instruction on how to be successful in academic oral or written English.

LEP: limited English proficient. This is the Every Student Succeeds Act Title III federal identifier for students who are learning English in addition to their native language. With the ESSA guidelines, LEP has changed to English learners; however, LEP continues to be a subgroup identifier.

EL? ELD? ESL?

EL = English learner

ELD = English language development

ESL = English as a second language, a program of service or a teaching certification or licensure

LM: language minority. Designation by some schools and states for ELs.

LT-EL: long-term ELs. Students who have been identified as LEP for five or more years. Many LT-ELs have been in U.S. schools since kindergarten and are natural-born citizens. Their English may sound fluent, but they have missed out on the development of academic language. The same is true when they read aloud: they sound fluent, but they have missed out on the development of reading comprehension skills. As a result of limited academic language and reading comprehension, their writing skills have not fully developed. The students' English language abilities are at risk of fossilizing unless explicit instruction is provided to ensure growth and success.

M-ELs: migrant English learners. Highly mobile in nature; may frequently move from school to school, state to state, or from their native home to the United States due to family or economic factors. ESL services and language instruction for migrant English learners is typically intermittent and disjointed because they travel from state to state when their parents follow the crop seasons to get jobs.

never-ELs. Monolingual English-speaking peers.

newcomer. At any grade level, students who arrive with little or no formal English language instruction. These learners typically identify as novice or beginning and enter the classroom at English language development level 1, Entering.

SIFE: students with interrupted formal education. Students who arrive at your school or classroom with a gap of two or more years of formal education. SIFE students need explicit instruction to help them recover the time missed in formal education as well as explicit English language instruction. Some SIFE students may never have attended school in a formal setting.

SLIFE. Students who enter the classroom with a gap of less than two years are, at times, referred to as SLIFE—students with *limited* or interrupted formal education.

refugees and unaccompanied minors. May be a part of the SIFE or SLIFE group but also need special services to help them through past or present trauma or daily struggles.

R-EL: reclassified English learners. ELs who have exited direct support, but still require services and as such are returned to LEP status with supporting documentation to that effect.

SpEd-EL: English learners with special educational needs. ELs with individual education programs (IEPs) or 504 plans. The IEP intervention team must consist of an ESL specialist if the student's disability is learning related. Special education services and LEP services are equally binding, and one does not supersede the other. Due diligence is required to correctly screen and identify these students based on learning disability and not language deficiency.

English Learner Related Terms

EFL: English as a foreign language. Those English language classes your students may have taken in their home or nonEnglish-speaking country. If you took Spanish, Japanese, German, or such in college, you will remember the typical format as a foreign language course.

ELD: English language development or English language development standards. A language-development progression developed by the WIDA consortium (www.wida.us) as based on a student's abilities in listening, speaking, reading, and writing. The ELD progression has six levels: entering (novice) to reaching (near native fluency). Some non-WIDA consortium states use their own state-defined ELD standards to assess their ELs.

ESL: English as a second language. According to the Department of Justice, ESL is a program of services provided to ELs. Nevertheless, ESL is sometimes labeled as a method, approach, component of instruction, or a subject of its own. It may also refer to a type of teacher licensure endorsement. It is not accurate when used as an identifier of ELs because ESL is a program of services, and an EL is a person. In Massachusetts and other states, it is a component of all the authorized programs, such as dual-language and sheltered instruction, but not as a stand-alone program.

ESOL: English for speakers of other languages. A program of service for ELs that may refer to a teacher licensure degree or endorsement.

ESP: English for special purposes. A subset of instruction specifically designed to instruct students in a skill or career. Many vocational schools and systems may use ESP to provide students with the needed terminology of mechanics, cosmetology, or other industries. ESP does not typically provide sufficient academic instructional depth to qualify as direct services under Title III and ESSA.

ExC-ELL: Expediting comprehension for English language learners. A whole-school, evidence-based professional development model based on twelve instructional components designed to facilitate successful acquisition of academic vocabulary, reading comprehension, and writing skills in all subject areas. ExC-ELL is for all teachers, coaches, and administrators in a school. In addition to the intensive training on instruction, coaches also undergo more training on how to coach ExC-ELL. Principals also attend all instructional sessions and their own focusing on how to support teachers and coaches as they implement ExC-ELL. This is bolstered by follow-up on-site coaching and administrative support.

RETELL: rethinking equity for teaching English language learners. A professional development program required for all core content teachers and administrators in the state of Massachusetts. The ExC-ELL professional model undergirds the RETELL components. Under department regulations adopted in June 2012, starting on July 1, 2016, core academic teachers (including preschool teachers) in public schools who are assigned to teach ELs must have a sheltered English instruction (SEI) endorsement or must earn the endorsement within one year of the assignment. Core academic teachers providing sheltered English instruction include: teachers of students with moderate disabilities; teachers of students with severe disabilities; subject-area teachers in English, reading, language arts, mathematics, science, civics and government, economics, history, and geography; and early childhood and elementary teachers who teach such content. Core academic teachers of ELs at Commonwealth charter schools are not required to hold an educator license, but they are subject to the same SEI endorsement requirements as core academic teachers of ELs in other public schools.

SCI: sheltered content instruction. Includes approaches, strategies, and methodology to make the content of lessons more comprehensible to the students and to promote the development of academic language needed to successfully master content standards. Sheltered content instruction (RETELL) must be taught by qualified content area teachers. Some states use the acronym SCI but create their own approaches.

SDAIE: specially designed academic instruction in English. Similar to SEI, a method for teaching ELs that is mainly used in California.

SEI: sheltered English immersion. Another method to teach English using second-language acquisition strategies for content areas. A licensure endorsement used by Massachusetts for core academic teachers and newly licensed educators based on sheltered English instruction strategies. Also another name for sheltered English instruction.

SEI: sheltered English instruction. English language instruction in the general education classroom by the content expert teacher using strategies devoted to teaching vocabulary, reading comprehension, and writing. Sheltered English instruction programs in Massachusetts serve ELs by providing both sheltered content-instruction and ESL instruction to support the rapid acquisition of English language proficiency by EL students as is required in Massachusetts's G. L. c. 71A and also to give them equal access to the general curricula taught in the schools.

TESOL: teaching English to speakers of other languages. A program of services provided to ELs. It may also refer to a type of teacher licensure endorsement.

WIDA: A consortium of states and groups formed to develop tools and assessments for the equity and success of ELs. Many states and educational institutions belong to this consortium and therefore WIDA ELD standards are used as a generic baseline for a student's English language development and progression.

REFERENCES AND RESOURCES

Adams, J. M. (2013, May 15). Social and emotional learning gaining new focus under Common Core. *EdSource*. Accessed at http://edsource.org/2013/social-and-emotional-learning-gaining-new-traction-under-common-core on May 16, 2016.

Aguilar, E., Goldwasser, D., & Tank-Crestetto, K. (2011). Support principals, transform schools. *Educational Leadership*, *69*(2), 70–73.

Alliance for Excellent Education. (2012, October). *The role of language and literacy in college- and career-ready standards: Rethinking policy and practice in support of English language learners.* Accessed at www.marylandpublicschools.org/cc/12.pdf on May 19, 2015.

August, D., Beck, I. L., Calderón, M., Francis, D. J., Lesaux, N. K., Shanahan, T., Erickson, F., Siegel L. S. (2008). Instruction and professional development. In D. August & T. Shanahan (Eds.), *Developing reading and writing in second language learners: Lessons from the Report of the National Literacy Panel on Language-Minority Children and Youth* (pp. 131–250). New York: Routledge.

August, D., & Calderón, M. (2006). Teacher beliefs and professional development. In D. August & T. Shanahan (Eds.), *Developing literacy in second-language learners: Report of the National Literacy Panel on Language-Minority Children and Youth* (pp. 555–565). Mahwah, NJ: Lawrence Erlbaum.

August, D., Carlo, M., Calderón, M., & Proctor, P. (2005). Development of literacy in Spanish-speaking English-language learners: Findings from a longitudinal study of elementary school children. *Perspectives*, *31*(2), 17–19.

August, D., & Shanahan, T. (Eds.). (2006). *Developing literacy in second-language learners: Report of the National Literacy Panel on Language-Minority Children and Youth.* Mahwah, NJ: Lawrence Erlbaum.

Beck, I. L., McKeown M. G., & Kucan, L. (2002). *Bringing words to life: Robust vocabulary instruction*. New York, NY: Guilford.

Beck, I. L., McKeown, M. G., & Kucan, L. (2005). Choosing words to teach. In E. H. Hiebert & M. L. Kamil (Eds.), *Teaching and learning vocabulary* (pp. 207–222). Mahwah, NJ: Lawrence Erlbaum.

Beyond Differences. (2016). *No one eats alone*. Accessed at www.nooneeatsalone.org/welcome/ on May 17, 2016.

Calderón, M. (1984). *Training bilingual trainers: An ethnographic study of coaching and its impact on the transfer of training.* (Doctoral dissertation). Retrieved from ProQuest Dissertations Publishing. (8616443)

Calderón, M. E. (1990). *Cooperative learning for limited English proficient students* (Distinguished scholar series). Austin: Texas Education Agency.

Calderón, M. E. (1991). Benefits of cooperative learning for Hispanic students. *Texas Research Journal, 2*, 39–57.

Calderón, M. (1994). Mentoring and coaching minority teachers. In R. A. De Villar & J. Cummings (Eds.), *Successful cultural diversity: Classroom practices for the 21st century.* New York: SUNY.

Calderón, M. (1996). La construcción de comunidades de aprendizaje para alumnos, maestros y directivos. *Sembrando: Revista de Educación de Jalisco, 1*(3), 5–7.

Calderón, M. (1999). Teachers Learning Communities for cooperation in diverse settings. In M. Calderón & R. E. Slavin (Eds.), *Building community through cooperative learning. Special issue of Theory into Practice Journal. 38*(2) p. 94–99. Columbus: The Ohio State University.

Calderón, M. E. (2007a). *Teaching reading to English language learners, grades 6–12: A framework for improving achievement in the content areas.* Thousand Oaks, CA: Corwin Press.

Calderón, M. E. (2007b). *RIGOR—Reading instructional goals for older readers: Reading program for 6th–12th students with interrupted formal education.* New York: Benchmark Education.

Calderón, M. E. (2009a). Language, literacy and knowledge for English language learners. *Better: Evidence-Based Education, 1*(1), 14–15.

Calderón, M. E. (2009b). Professional development: Continuing to understand how to teach children from diverse backgrounds. In L. M. Morrow, R. Rueda, & D. Lapp (Eds.), *Handbook of literacy and research on literacy instruction: Issues of diversity, policy and equity* (pp. 413–430). New York: Guilford Press.

Calderón, M. E. (2010). *Expediting reading comprehension for English language learners: A five-year study*. New York: Carnegie Corporation of New York.

Calderón, M. E. (2010–2014). *Recommendations for the Boston Public Schools on the instruction of English learners: Reports to the United States Department of Justice*. Washington, DC: United States Department of Justice.

Calderón, M. E. (2011a). *Teaching reading and comprehension to English learners, K–5*. Bloomington, IN: Solution Tree Press.

Calderón, M. E. (2011b). Teaching writing to ELLs in high schools. *Better: Evidence-Based Education, 3*(2), 8–9.

Calderón, M. E. (Ed.). (2012). *Breaking through: Effective instruction and assessment for reaching English learners*. Bloomington, IN: Solution Tree Press.

Calderón, M. E., August, D., Slavin, A., Cheung, A., Duran, D., & Madden, N. (2005). Bringing words to life in classrooms with English-language learners. In E. H. Hiebert & M. Kamil (Eds.), *Teaching and learning vocabulary: Bringing research to practice* (pp. 115–136). Mahwah, NJ: Lawrence Erlbaum.

Calderón, M. E., Carreón, A., Cantú, J., & Minaya-Rowe, L. (2010). *Expediting comprehension for English language learners: Participants' manual*. New York: Benchmark Education.

Calderón, M., Hertz-Lazarowitz, R., Ivory, G., & Slavin, R. E. (February 1997). *Effects of Bilingual Cooperative Integrated Reading and Composition (BCIRC) on students transitioning from Spanish to English* (Report No. 10). Baltimore, MD: Center for Research on the Education of Students Placed at Risk, Johns Hopkins University.

Calderón, M. E., Hertz-Lazarowitz, R., & Slavin, R. E. (1998). Effects of bilingual cooperative integrated reading and composition on students making the transition from Spanish to English reading. *Elementary School Journal, 99*(2), 153–165.

Calderón M. E., & Minaya-Rowe, L. (2011). *Preventing long-term ELs: Transforming schools to meet core standards*. Thousand Oaks, CA: Corwin Press.

Calderón, M. E., & Slakk, S. S. (2016). *Expediting Comprehension for English Language Learners (ExC-ELL): Teachers' and administrators' manual*. Washington, DC: Margarita Calderón & Associates.

Calderón, M. E. & Soto, I. (2016). *Academic language mastery: Vocabulary in context*. Thousand Oaks, CA: Corwin Press.

Calderón, M. E., Trejo, M., & Montenegro, H. (2016). *Literacy strategies for English learners in core content secondary classrooms*. Bloomington, IN: Solution Tree Press.

Carlo, M. S., August, D., & Snow, C. E. (2005). Sustained vocabulary-learning strategy instruction for English language learners. In E. H. Hiebert & M. L. Kamil (Eds.), *Teaching and learning vocabulary: Bringing research to practice* (pp. 137–154). Mahwah, NJ: Lawrence Erlbaum.

Collaborative for Academic, Social, and Emotional Learning. (2013). *CASEL schoolkit: A guide for implementing schoolwide academic, social, and emotional learning*. Unpublished manuscript, Collaborative for Academic, Social and Emotional Learning, Chicago.

Collaborative for Academic, Social, and Emotional Learning. (2016, February). CASEL Cross-Districts Learning Event, Reno, NV.

Collier, V. P. & Thomas, W. P. (2004). The astounding effectiveness of dual language education for all. *NABE Journal of Research and Practice*, *2*(1), 1–20.

Committee on the Study of Teacher Preparation Programs in the United States. (2010). *Preparing teachers: Building evidence for sound policy*. Washington, DC: National Research Council.

Crowley, B., & Saide, B. (2016, January 20). Building empathy in classrooms and schools. *Education Week*. Accessed at www.edweek.org /tm/articles/2016/01/20/building-empathy-in-classrooms-and-schools .html on May 17, 2016.

Darling-Hammond, L. (2009). *Thoughts on teacher preparation*. San Rafael, CA. Edutopia, The George Lucas Educational Foundation.

Deshler, D. D., Palincsar, A. S., Biancarosa, G., & Nair, M. (2007). *Informed choices for struggling adolescent readers*. Newark, DE: International Reading Association.

Devine, M., Meyers, R., & Houssemand, C. (2013). How can coaching make a positive impact within educational settings? *Procedia: Social and Behavioral Sciences*, *93*, 1382–1389. Accessed at www.sciencedirect .com/science/article/pii/S1877042813034939 on May 17, 2016.

DuFour, R., (May 2004). What is a professional learning community? *Educational Leadership*, *61*(8), 6–11.

Durlak, J. A., Weissberg, R. P., Dymnicki, A. B., Taylor, R. D., & Schellinger, K. B. (2011). The impact of enhancing students' social and emotional learning: A meta-analysis of school-based universal interventions. *Child Development*, *82*(1), 405–432.

Elias, M. J., & Arnold, H. (Eds.). (2006). *The educator's guide to emotional intelligence and academic achievement: Social-emotional learning in the classroom.* Thousand Oaks, CA: Corwin Press.

Elias, M. J., Zins, J. E., Weissberg, R. P., Frey, K. S., Greenberg, M. T., Haynes, N. M., . . . Shriver, T. P. (1997). *Promoting social and emotional learning: Guidelines for educators.* Alexandria, VA: Association for Supervision and Curriculum Development.

Every Student Succeeds Act of 2015, 114th Congress § 1177 (2016).

Fullan, M. (2002, May). The change leader. *Educational Leadership, 59*(8), 16–21.

Fullan, M. (2008). *The six secrets of change: What the best leaders do to help their organizations survive and thrive.* San Francisco: Jossey-Bass.

Fullan, M. (2014). *The principal: Three keys to maximizing impact.* San Francisco: Jossey-Bass.

Gándara, P. (2005). *Listening to teachers of English learners: A survey of California teachers' challenges, experiences and professional development needs.* Santa Barbara, CA: Language Minority Research Institute.

Garet, M. S., Cronen, S., Eaton, M., Kurki, A., Ludwig, M., Jones, W., . . . Sztejnberg, L. (2008). *The impact of two professional development interventions on early reading instruction and achievement.* Washington, DC: U.S. Department of Education.

Goleman, D. (1995). *Emotional intelligence: Why it can matter more than IQ.* New York: Bantam.

Gonzalez, V., Yawkey, T., & Minaya-Rowe, L. (2006). *English-as-a-second-language (ESL) teaching and learning: Classroom applications for Pre-K-12th grade students.* Needham Heights, MA: Allyn & Bacon.

Graham, S., & Hebert, M. (2010). *Writing to read: Evidence for how writing can improve reading—A report from Carnegie Corporation of New York.* Washington, DC: Alliance for Excellent Education.

Graves, M. F. (2006). *The vocabulary book: Learning and instruction.* New York: Teachers College Press.

Graves, M., August, D., & Carlo, M. (2011). Teaching 50,000 words. *Better: Evidence-Based Education, 3*(2), 6–7. Accessed at http://esl .ncwiseowl.org/UserFiles/Servers /Server_4502383/File/all.pdf on May 17, 2016.

Gregoire, C. (2015, March 5). 5 surprising ways mindfulness can change you. *Huffington Post.* Accessed at www.huffingtonpost .com/2015/03/05/surprising-mindfulness-be_n_6771374.html on May 17, 2016.

Guskey, T. R. (October 2010). Lessons of mastery learning. *Educational Leadership, 68*(2), 52–57.

Hargreaves, A., & Fullan, M. (2012). *Professional capital: Transforming teaching in every school.* New York: Teachers College Press.

Hill, L. (2005, December). *Leadership development: A strategic imperative for higher education* (Harvard Business School Working Paper No. 06–023). Accessed at http://net.educause.edu/ir/library/pdf/FFP0506S.pdf on December 4, 2012.

Igoa, C. (1995). *The inner world of the immigrant child.* Mahwah, NJ: Lawrence Erlbaum Associates.

Joyce, B., & Showers, B. (1996). Staff development as a comprehensive service organization. *Journal of Staff Development, 17*(1), 2–6.

Joyce, B., & Showers, B. (2002). *Student achievement through staff development* (3rd ed.). Alexandria, VA: Association for Supervision and Curriculum Development.

Kamil, M. L., & Hiebert, E. H. (Eds.). (2005). *Teaching and learning vocabulary: Bringing research to practice.* Mahwah, NJ: Lawrence Erlbaum Associates, Inc.

Kise, J. A. G. (2014). *Unleashing the positive power of differences: Polarity thinking in our schools.* Thousand Oaks, CA: Corwin Press.

Knight, J. (2011). *Unmistakable impact: A partnership approach for dramatically improving instruction.* Thousand Oaks, CA: Corwin Press.

Knight, J. (2012). *High-impact instruction. A framework for great teaching.* Thousand Oaks: Corwin Press.

Kouzes, J. M., & Posner, B. Z. (2012). *The leadership challenge: How to make extraordinary things happen in organizations* (5th ed.). San Francisco: Jossey-Bass.

Lantieri, L. (2015). *Mindfulness practice during a CASEL webinar for the School Guide for Systemic SEL Implementation.* Chicago: Author.

Limited English Proficiency. (n.d.). *Commonly asked questions and answers regarding limited english proficient (LEP) individuals.* Accessed at www.lep.gov/faqs/faqs.html#OneQ1 on May 18, 2016.

Marsh, D., & Calderón, M. (1989). Applying research on effective bilingual instruction in a multi-district inservice teacher training program. *National Association for Bilingual Education Journal, 12*(1), 133–152.

McGroarty, M., & Calderón, M. E. (2005). Cooperative learning for second language learners: Models, applications and challenges. In P. A. Richard-Amato & M. A. Snow (Eds.), *Academic success for English language learners: Strategies for K–12 mainstream teachers* (pp. 174–194). White Plains, NY: Longman.

Nagy, W. (2005). Why vocabulary instruction needs to be long-term and comprehensive. In E. H. Hiebert & M. L. Kamil (Eds.), *Teaching and learning vocabulary: Bringing research to practice* (pp. 27–44). Mahwah, NJ: Lawrence Erlbaum.

National Governors Association Center for Best Practices & Council of Chief State School Officers. (2010a). *Common Core State Standards for English language arts and literacy in history/social studies, science, and technical subjects.* Washington, DC: Authors. Accessed at www.corestandards.org/assets/CCSSI_ELA%20Standards.pdf on November 6, 2016.

National Governors Association Center for Best Practices & Council of Chief State School Officers. (2010b). *Common Core State Standards for mathematics.* Washington, DC: Authors. Accessed at www.corestandards.org/assets/CCSSI_Math%20Standards.pdf on November 6, 2016.

National Reading Panel. (2000). *Teaching children to read: An evidence-based assessment of the scientific research literature on reading and its implications for reading instruction.* Washington, DC: National Institute of Child Health and Human Development.

National Research Council. (2010). *Preparing teachers: Building evidence for sound policy.* Washington, DC: The National Academies Press.

No Child Left Behind Act of 2001, 20 U.S. C. § 6319 (2008).

Padrón, Y. N., Waxman, H. C., & Rivera, H. H. (2002). Issues in educating Hispanic students. In S. Stringfield & D. Land (Eds.), *Educating at-risk students* (pp. 66–88). Chicago: National Society for the Study of Education.

Pashler, H., Bain, P., Bottge, B., Graesser, A., Koedinger, K., McDaniel, M., & Metcalfe, J. (2007). *Organizing instruction and study to improve student learning* (NCER 2007-2004). Washington, DC: National Center for Education Research, Institute of Education Sciences, U.S. Department of Education. Accessed at http://ies.ed.gov/nree/wwc/pdf/practiceguides/20072004.pdf on October 14, 2016.

Reading Rockets. (n.d.). *Vocabulary.* Accessed at www.readingrockets.org/reading-topics/vocabulary on May 18, 2016.

Rick's Resources. (2016). *Kindness task cards.* Accessed at www
.teacherspayteachers.com/Product/Kindness-Task-Cards-48-Social
-Skills-738305 on May 18, 2016.

Samuels, S. J. (2002). Reading fluency: Its development and assessment.
In Pacific Resources for Education and Learning (Ed.) *Readings on
fluency for "A focus on fluency forum."* Honolulu, HI: PREL.

Sapon-Shevin, M. (2010). *Because we can change the world: A practical
guide to building cooperative, inclusive classroom communities* (2nd ed.).
Boston: Allyn & Bacon.

Saunders, W., Goldenberg, C., & Marcelletti, D. (2013). English language
development: Guidelines for instruction. *American Educator, 37*(2),
13–25, 38–39.

Schaps, E., Battistich, V., & Solomon, D. (2004). Community in school
as key to student growth: Findings from the child development project.
In J. E. Zins, R. P. Weissberg, M. C. Wang, & H. J. Walberg (Eds.),
*Building academic success on social and emotional learning: What does the
research say?* (pp. 189–207). New York: Teachers College Press.

Senge, P., Cambron-McCabe, N., Lucas, T., Smith, B., & Dutton, J.
(2012). *Schools that learn: A fifth discipline fieldbook for educators,
parents and everyone who cares about education* (5th ed.). New York:
Doubleday.

Short, D. J., & Fitzsimmons, S. (2007). *Double the work: Challenges
and solutions to acquiring language and academic literacy for adolescent
English language learners.* Washington, DC: Alliance for Excellent
Education.

Slavin, R. E. (1995). *Cooperative learning: Theory, research, and practice*
(2nd ed.). Boston: Allyn & Bacon.

Slavin, R. E., Madden, N., Calderón, M., Chamberlain, A., & Hennessy,
M. (2009). *Reading and language outcomes of a randomized evaluation
of transitional bilingual education.* Washington, DC: Institute of
Education Sciences, U.S. Department of Education.

Smith, D., Fisher, D., & Frey, N. (2015). *Better than carrots or sticks:
Restorative practices for positive classroom management.* Alexandria, VA:
Association for Supervision and Curriculum Development.

Snow, K. E. (Ed.). (2002). *Reading for understanding: Toward an R &
D program in reading comprehension.* Santa Monica, CA: RAND
Corporation.

Strickland, D. S., & Alvermann, D. E. (Eds.). (2004). *Bridging the literacy
achievement gap grades 4 to 12.* New York: Teachers College Press.

Thomas, W. P., & Collier, V. (1997). *School Effectiveness for Language Minority Students*. Washington, DC: Disseminated by National Clearinghouse for Bilingual Education, the George Washington University, Center for the Study of Language and Education.

U.S. Department of Education. (2015). *Schools' civil rights obligations to English learner students and limited English proficient parents*. Accessed at www2.ed.gov/about/offices/list/ocr/ellresources.html on May 18, 2016.

U.S. Department of Education. (2016). *Newcomer tool kit*. Accessed at www2.ed.gov/about/offices/list/oela/newcomers-toolkit/index.html on November 29, 2016.

U.S. Department of Justice. (2010). *Successor settlement agreement between the United States of American and the Boston Public Schools*. Accessed at www.justice.gov/sites/default/files/crt/legacy/2012/04/25/bostonsuccessoragree.pdf on November 4, 2016.

U.S. Department of Justice, Civil Rights Division, & U.S. Department of Education, Office for Civil Rights. (2015a). *Ensuring English learner students can participate meaningfully and equally in educational programs*. Accessed at www2.ed.gov/about/offices/list/ocr/docs/dcl-factsheet-el-students-201501.pdf on May 18, 2016.

U.S. Department of Justice, Civil Rights Division, & U.S. Department of Education, Office for Civil Rights. (2015b). [Dear colleague letter about education and Title VI of the Civil Rights Act of 1964]. Accessed at www2.ed.gov/about/offices/list/ocr/letters/colleague-el-201501.pdf on May 18, 2016.

Valdes, G. (1997) Dual-language immersion programs: A cautionary note concerning the education of language-minority students. *Harvard Educational Review, 67*(3), 391–430.

Vygotsky, L. (1978). *Mind in society. The development of higher psychological processes*. Cambridge, MA: Harvard University Press.

Walqui, A., & van Lier, L. (2010). *Scaffolding the academic success of adolescent English language learners: A pedagogy of promise*. San Francisco: WestEd. Accessed at http://www.WestEd.org/scaffoldingacademicsuccess on May 8, 2016.

Zins, J. E., Weissberg, R. P., Wang, M. C., & Walberg, H. J. (Eds.). (2004). *Building academic success on social and emotional learning: What does the research say?* New York: Teachers College Press.

INDEX

Breaking Through
Edited by Margarita Espino Calderón
Utilizing research and field studies, this book outlines a whole-school approach to helping English learners achieve. Discover how integrating language, literacy, and subject matter instruction leads to greater success for this growing student population.
BKF552

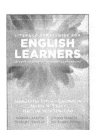

Literacy Strategies for English Learners in Core Content Secondary Classrooms
Margarita Espino Calderón, Maria N. Trejo, and Hector Montenegro
Motivate English learners to boost proficiency with confidence. Working within the framework of the Common Core and other state standards, this book focuses on instructional strategies that integrate language, literacy, and content across subject areas to ensure all students thrive.
BKF615

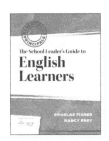

The School Leader's Guide to English Learners
Douglas Fisher and Nancy Frey
English learners face a difficult challenge: learning in English. How, then, do you set reasonable expectations for developing proficiency? School leaders will learn how to assess the individual needs of ELs, how to create a quality instructional program, and how to evaluate performance.
BKF540

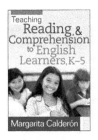

Teaching Reading & Comprehension to English Learners, K–5
Margarita Espino Calderón
Raise achievement for English learners through new instructional strategies and assessment processes. This book addresses the language, literacy, and content instructional needs of ELs and frames quality instruction within effective schooling structures and the implementation of RTI.
BKF402

Printed in the USA
CPSIA information can be obtained
at www.ICGtesting.com
LVHW081256111023
760311LV00001B/3